GW01280488

H. U. JOHNSON.

FROM
DIXIE TO CANADA

ROMANCES AND REALITIES

OF THE

UNDERGROUND RAILROAD

BY

H. U. JOHNSON

AUTHOR OF "SEVENTEEN SEVENTY-SIX AND OTHER POEMS"
AND "OBED IN THE GREAT CO-PARTNERSHIP."

VOL. I

FIRST THOUSAND

PRYOR PUBLICATIONS
WHITSTABLE AND WYRLEY

PRYOR PUBLICATIONS
WHITSTABLE AND WYRLEY

Specialist in Facsimile Reproductions

MEMBER OF
INDEPENDENT PUBLISHERS GUILD

75 Dargate Road, Yorkletts, Whitstable,
Kent CT5 3AE, England
Tel. & Fax: (01227) 274655

E-mail: alan@pryor-publications.co.uk
www.pryor-publications.co.uk

Kent Exporter of the Year Awards Winner 1998/2000

Every effort has been made to trace copyright ownership
©Pryor Publications 2002
©H. U. Johnson

ISBN 0 946014 64 7

A full list of Titles sent free on request

First Published in 1894
By Charles Wells Moulton

Printed and bound
by
Estudios Gráficos ZURE, S.A.
48950 - Erandio (Spain)

DEDICATION.

TO the millions of happy grand-children of a generation fast leaving the stage of action, and who must get their knowledge of the Rebellion and its causes from the lips of those who saw and participated or from the pages of history, as we, the grand-parents, got ours of the Revolution from those long since passed away, and from the written records of that thrilling period, this little volume of unique but wonderful history is sincerely and most affectionately dedicated by one of the Grandfathers.

PREFACE.

THE years intervening since the abolition of American slavery leave a majority of our peo-people ignorant of its workings, and of matters connected with it, except as they are gleaned from the pages of history, or from the lips of those now grown old.

It is not the purpose of this little volume to discuss the history of the "peculiar institution" in detail, but simply to give so much of it as will make appreciable the cause for another one equally "peculiar," known for the last twenty years of its existence as the UNDERGROUND RAILROAD,—a name for a mode of operation, and not of a corporation or material object.

During the years of its operation, secrecy was a cardinal, an imperative principle of its management, as the following pages will make apparent. On the breaking out of the War of the Rebellion, thus putting an end to its operations, every other subject was swallowed up in the excitement of the great struggle, and subsequently in that of Reconstruction. Thus the Road dropped measurably out of sight, leaving but meager reports and archives to tell the story of its working.

The promptings of a desire to leave to posterity some realistic record of this, one of the most wonderful and thrilling features of our national history, no parallel to which is afforded in the annals of time, must be the excuse for these pages. During the eighties, the writer, who had lived amid its excitements for years, and was more or less familiar with the writings of Coffin, Pettit, the Clarkes and others, undertook a systematic research into the matter, the result of which was the accumulation of a large fund of incident and information pertaining to the Road, much of which was published in the *Home Magazine* between the years 1883 and 1889, inclusive. Those articles, in part, carefully revised, are now placed before the reader in this more permanent form, with the hope that they may receive the generous approval of an appreciative public.

THE AUTHOR.

ORWELL, OHIO, MAY 20, 1894.

CONTENTS.

	PAGE
INTRODUCTION	9

CHAPTER I.
JO NORTON	19
LAVINIA	28
A RUSE	36
THE ORIGINAL "JERRY"	48
A COOL WOMAN	52

CHAPTER II.
JACK WATSON	54

CHAPTER III.
UNCLE JAKE	85

CHAPTER VI.
GEORGE GREEN, OR CONSTANCY REWARDED.	98

CHAPTER V.
HOW SOL. JONES WAS LEFT	124

CHAPTER VI.
EDWARD HOWARD	132

CHAPTER VII.
PLUCKY CHARLEY	152

CHAPTER VIII.
STATIE LINES	164

CHAPTER IX.
GEORGE GRAY	173

JIM JONES IN THE BLACKSMITH SHOP.

INTRODUCTION.

THE quiet of a midsummer night had settled down over the city of Washington, when, in August, 1839, a dusky form came, with stealthy tread, from among some buildings not far away, and cautiously approached the eastern entrance to the Capitol. Laying his hand upon the cold steps in the shadow of the great building, Jim Jones, a colored boy of about seventeen, attentively listened as if in expectation of some preconcerted signal.

He had waited but a moment thus, when the hand of a patrol was laid heavily upon his shoulder and the rough query, "What does this mean, you black rascal?" fell upon his ear.

"Dunno, Massa," was the reply of the startled boy.

"Don't know, you black imp?"

"No, Massa, dunno what fo' I was hea."

"Well, you know, you young nigger, you have no business here at this hour of the night."

"Yes, Massa, I knowed de night am for white folks, and I jus, cum for to see—"

"Some d—d abolitionist who is trying to get you away."

"No, no, Massa."

"Well, come along and we shall see," saying which he rudely hurried the boy away to a place of safe keeping.

In the early morning Jim was recognized by his master, who vainly tried to extort from him by questioning the cause of his nocturnal ramble. Failing in this, the boy was taken to a blacksmith shop and his thumbs placed end to end in the jaws of a vice.

"Now," said the master, "tell me why you were abroad last night."

"I dunno," replied Jim.

A half turn of the screw, and a groan of pain escaped the boy; another turn and he writhed in agony.

"Now you black son of a b——ch, why were you at the Capitol last night?"

"O Lor', Massa, a white man tol' me I should come."

"What did he want of you?"

"Fo' to go norf'."

"And so you were going?"

"Y-e-s—Massa—I-was-fo'-to-go."

"How?"

"On a railroad undah de groun'."

"Under the ground?"

"Yes, Massa, so the gem'an said. He was jus' comin' to open de way, when Massa da' cotched me."

"Who was he?"

"Dunno, Massa."

Another turn of the screw, and in the agony of despair the boy yelled, "Dunno, dunno, Massa, dunno," and swooned away.

After resuscitation the torture was again applied, but nothing farther was elicited, as the boy continued to aver he had never heard the name of the man who was to lead him ; and, indeed, he had met him only in the dark.

Though for years slaves had from time to time been stealing away from the *kind* attentions of their masters, and, indeed, very frequently of late, yet never before had the latter dreamed that their " chattel went by subterranean transit, and the theme became one of such absorbing interest that, when two months later five prominent slaves escaped from the city in a single night, a Washington morning paper heralded the matter before the world for the first time as follows:—

"UNDERGROUND RAILROAD!
A Mystery Not Yet Solved."

"The abolition incendiaries are undermining, not only our domestic institutions, but the very foundations of our Capitol. Our citizens will recollect that the boy Jim, who was arrested last August, while lurking about the Capitol, would disclose nothing until he was subject to torture by screwing his fingers in a blacksmith's vice, when he acknowledged that he was to have been sent north by railroad; was to have started near the place where he stood when discovered by the patrol. He refused to tell who was to aid him—said he did not know—and most likely he did not. Nothing more could be got from him until they gave the screw another turn, when he said : '*The railroad goes under ground all the way to Boston.*' Our citizens are losing all their best servants. Some secret Yankee arrangement has been contrived by which they 'stampede' from three to eight at a time, and no trace of them can be found until they reach the interior of New York or the New England States. They can not have gone by railroad, as every station is closely watched by a secret police, yet there is no other conveyance by which a man can reach Albany in two days. That they have done so, is now clearly demonstrated. Colonel Hardy, a tobacco planter residing in the District, about five miles from the city, lost five more slaves last Sunday evening. They were pursued by an expert slave catcher, but no trace of them was discovered. The search was abandoned this morning, the Colonel having received a paper called the *Liberty Press*, printed in Albany, with the following article so marked as to claim his attention:

"'Arrived, this morning, by our fast train, three men and two women. They were claimed as slaves by Colonel Hardy, of the District of Columbia, but became dissatisfied with the Colonel's ways of *bucking* Harry, making *love* to Nancy and other similar displays of *masterly* affection, and left the old fellow's premises last Sunday evening, arriving at our station by the quickest passage on record.'

"The article recites many incidents that have transpired in the Colonel's family, that correspond so exactly with facts that the Colonel says: 'Nobody but Kate could have told that story!' Said article closes by saying: 'Now, Colonel H., please give yourself no trouble about these friends of yours, for they will be safe under the protection of the British Lion before this *meets* your eyes.'"

The term which had been given to poor Jim, in confidence, as the means by which he was to make his escape from bondage, and extorted from him by torture, having thus been given to the world from the city of Washington, became henceforth the universal appelation for a *corporation* which, for more than twenty years thereafter, extended its great trunk

INTRODUCTION.

lines across all the northern states from Mason and Dixon's line and the Ohio River to the Queen's Dominion, and its ramifications far into the southern states. It was most efficiently officered, and had its side tracks, connections and switches; its stations and eating houses all thoroughly well recognized by the initiated; its station agents and conductors, men undaunted in danger and unswerving in their adherence to principle; its system of cypher dispatches, tokens and nomenclature which no attache ever revealed except to those having a right to receive them, and its detective force characterized by a shrewdness in expedients and a versatility of strategy which attached to any mere money making enterprise would have put " millions in it." It received the support of men and women from every class, sect, and party, though from some more than from others; its character was engraven, as by a pen of fire, in the hearts and consciences of men, burning deeper and deeper, until finally abrogated in that grand emancipation proclamation of Abraham Lincoln, when it was found that its stock, always unwatered but by tears, had yielded an incomputable percentage in the freedom secured to over thirty-six thousand fugitives from human bondage, and embodied in houses, lands, schools, churches and social and domestic happiness.

Now that the track is all pulled up; that the rolling stock has disappeared; that most of the operators and passengers have gone down into silence or are dwelling in forgetfulness of accumulating years, and that only a few of the old stations remain as they were, a new generation pertinently inquires, "What called such a road into existence and how were its gigantic operations so successfully and yet so secretly carried on?"

To the first of these questions it may be replied that the history of American slavery is older than the story of Plymouth Rock. In the year 1619 a cargo of Africans, kidnapped on the coast of the "Dark Continent," was sold from the deck of a Dutch man-of-war at Jamestown, Va., to be used in the cultivation of tobacco along the river.

At that time very little was thought about the enormity of human slavery. The labor proved remunerative, and the institution spread over the original colonies, with little or no question, so that at the breaking out of the Revolution there were 500,000 bondmen, a standing menace to the cause of freedom, and yet technically said to be "armed in the holy cause of liberty."

On the adoption of the constitution in 1787, public sentiment had become so strong against the African slave trade that provision was made for its abolition in 1808. Persistent effort was also made, particularly by the Quakers, for the ultimate abolition of slavery itself, but without avail, as it was claimed by its apologists that it would ultimately die of its own accord—a prophecy in some sense fulfilled, though in a manner all undreamed by those who made it.

INTRODUCTION. 15

Though Anti-slavery Societies had long been in vogue, of one of which Benjamin Franklin had been president, it was found by the census of 1800 that the country contained 893,000 slaves. From this time forward one after another of the Northern States abolished it, until it finally disappeared from New York last of all, July 4th, 1827. In the meantime it was strengthened in the South. The invention of the cotton gin and the extensive manufacture of sugar in the Gulf States, made the rearing of slaves in those farther north very lucrative, and slave marts were set up in many of their cities and towns to which men, women and children were brought and sold upon the auction block and at private sale.

The slaves thus purchased in Maryland, Virginia, Kentucky and elsewhere for the more southern markets were either driven across the country like so many cattle, or, if more convenient, taken down the Ohio and Mississippi on steam-boats or in flats, all those deemed likely to give trouble being handcuffed together across a coffle chain, thus constituting a "coffle."

On their arrival at the place of destination, they were more or less jaded and warm, and hence unmarketable until properly fitted up. To facilitate this, buildings or "pens" were provided where they were well fed and given liberal rations of whiskey. Under the management of some genial dealer, they were induced to tell stories, sing songs and make merry. In this way they were soon recuperated and ready for the ordeals of another sale in which they were subjected to much the same scrutiny of body and limb that is bestowed upon a horse when the person would ascertain its physical condition.

To escape this degradation and the hardships of the southern plantations, the more intelligent and hardy of the slave population early began to flee to the free states as an asylum from cruel bondage. As if in anticipation of this, the constitution had provided for their return, and under its provisions many were restored to their masters, through the cupidity of sordid northern men, for the rewards offered.

Finding so many of their chattels escaping and the sentiment against their return growing stronger and stronger, the southern people, with the aid of abettors at the north, succeeded in 1850, in securing the passage of the Fugitive Slave-law, which imposed heavy fines and even imprisonment for in any way aiding a fugitive from slavery to escape. By its provisions every man at the North was virtually made a slave-catcher.

Canada now became the goal of the fugitive, and to its safe retreat thousands escaped, and yet so successful was the business of slave culture that in 1860 the whole number of persons held as mere chattels, without a vested right in land, or home, or wife, or husband, or child, or life, even, that might not be served by the will of the master, amounted to 3,953,000 souls. The bitterness of sectional feeling engendered by such a state of affairs, and the intense

INTRODUCTION.

activity of nerve and intellect called forth thereby, can never be duly appreciated except by those who were active participants in the affairs of ten years *ante bellum.*

The second question, and, also, many points covered by the first, will be best answered by following the thread of these "Romances and Realties of the Underground Railrood," gathered as they are from personal observation, extensive reading, visitations along many of the old lines, and numerous interviews and extensive correspondence with those heroic men and women who dared their fortunes and their personal liberty in the cause of humanity and right, still lingering among us, as, also, with many a passenger over this truly wonderful thoroughfare.

REFUGEES IN WASHINGTON CHURCHYARD.

CHAPTER I.

JO NORTON.

I.

SO many and varied have been the changes of half a century, and so rapid the growth of the city in the past twenty-five years, that few of the present inhabitants of Washington, and less of its old-time frequenters, now ever think of the cemetery that skirted the stage road leading north from the city. True, in those by-gone days it was a popular burial place, even for the first families of the capital, but like many another "silent city" it long since fell into disuse, and consequently became for years the most desirable place near the city for an underground railroad station, and to such use it was assiduously appropriated.

In this solitary place, on a quiet Sabbath evening of October, 1839, there was heard just as the last faint twilight trembled on the western horizon a low, distinct whistle. Immediately there arose from among the growth of bushes and from behind already reclining headstones five dusky forms, actuated evidently by the same impulse. The whistle was repeated, and the forms cautiously approached the point whence it proceeded, and there gathered in presence of a stranger to them all, but with no previous knowledge of each other's intent, though all of them were the property of the same man, Colonel Hardy, a tobacco planter of the District of Columbia, as previously stated in the "Introduction" to these "Romances and Realities."

The first exclamations of surprise over, their unknown companion proceeded to give them the instructions for the night, after allaying their superstitious fears, that they were to sink into the earth for a time, and be under the conduct of invisible personages. Indeed, so far from that being the case they soon found very much depended upon their own physical exertion. No sinking down into the ground among the dead, no sojourn among spooks and ghosts, impressions that had almost gotten the better of their thirst for freedom, was to be theirs. On the contrary they were to take at once to the pike and follow it until they came to the said road, which was then to be their pathway, only turning out to pass around villages and stations until they came to a man standing in the track who should signal them by the simple name "Ben." To him they were to yield themselves implicitly.

Seeing the little company once fairly started, the stranger returned to the city, and as he passed the postoffice deposited therein a letter addressed,

"*JOHN JONES, Esq.,*
Albany,
N. Y."

Leaving this missive and the fugitives to pursue their respective journeys, we pause to inquire into the personalities of the latter. They were named, respectively, Nancy, Kate, Robert, Harry and Jo, or more complete, Jo Norton.

As has been said, they were the property of one man, and when not needed on the plantation, were hired out in the city. Harry was recognized among his fellows as a man of spirit and ability; but the latter quality never saved him from the frequent "buckings" engendered by the two free play of the former. Nancy, an octaroon, was well formed, about twenty years of age, and according to Kate, who had a spontaneous gift of gossip, a special favorite of the "Kunnel."

Jo Norton was a sprighty, intelligent fellow, and had a wife named Mary, who, with their little boy, was the property of a Mr. Judson, residing in the city. In his boyhood Jo had been continually employed upon the plantation, but after he was sixteen was engaged at a hotel during the winter for several years. For a long time in this place it was his special duty to wait upon Daniel Webster at table and otherwise. It was whilst thus employed that he became acquainted with and won Mary, who had the care of the great statesman's rooms. During the summer, the Colonel, when reasonably good natured, allowed Jo to visit his wife and child once in two weeks, on Sunday. When too choleric to grant his "chattel" this indulgence, a pass was readily secured from the old man's daughter, who was his private secretary, and with whom Jo was a great favorite. In these visits the possibility of an escepe, more especially for the sake of their boy, was frequently discussed, though no plan was ever perfected.

One evening whilst returning from one of these visitations, Jo fell in company with a gentleman whose manner so impressed him that he asked if he were not from " de Norf.".

" Yes, from Massachusetts," said the stranger.

"Wy, Massa, dat am de home ob de great Dan'l Webster."

" Yes; I know him very well."

" Yes, Massa, an' doan dis chile knows dat great man to?"

" How is that?"

"Wy, Massa, doan I stan' 'hind his chaah all dese winters wen him comes to Congress?"

" Ah, I see. But wouldn't you like to go north and be free?"

" Lor' Massa, dat was wat Mary and I talks 'bout dis blessed day."

" Who is Mary?"

" Mary am my wife, sah, and James am my little boy. Da'longs to anuder man."

"A wife and child!" said the stranger half musingly. " Well my good fellow, we will see what can be done, but we must talk no more now. Meet me on the corner of "F" and the Avenue two weeks from to-day at noon."

"Yes sah," and the two parted.

Two weeks passed, and, as agreed, the parties met, the one readily assuming the air of a southern gentleman and the other instinctively falling into the role of his servant. Thus they passed on until a quiet place was reached, when it was agreed that Jo should take a designated place in the old cemetery three weeks from that night, but that Mary and the child should be left in the city till a fitting way for their escape presented itself. In the mean time the other parties had been separately interviewed, and assigned their several hiding places, and given the signal which would call them into the presence of a stranger. Thus it was that they came together unawares.

II.

Once upon the public highway the little party struck out briskly for the railroad upon which they turned their faces towards Baltimore, and following their instructions were making fine progress, when, about midnight, as they were passing around a village the heavens became suddenly overcast with clouds, and for an hour or more they wandered in uncertainty. A halt being called, a lively discussion based upon five different opinions arose, and how it might have terminated no one can tell had not the heavens just then cleared up, enabling Harry, who was both conductor to and astronomer for the train, to get their bearings from "de ol' norf." So much time had thus been lost that daybreak was just beginning to tinge the east when the mystical word "Ben" fell from the lips of a man standing upon the track, whom they at once followed for some distance into a corn-field, where he removed several bundels from a stack of corn-fodder, and the two women entered a "dodger" apartment, whilst the men were similarly secreted a little farther on.

A thirty mile walk had given them a good appetite for the bountiful breakfast provided, after partaking of which they lay down and slept soundly, whilst "Old Ben," a free negro who had been furnished the means to rent and till this field and arrange it as a "way station," kept constant vigil and obliterated their tracks by husking corn and carefully drawing the stocks over them.

III.

Morning came in the city, and soon the absence of the servants from their employers was reported at the plantation, where the non-appearance of Jo had already caused the Colonel to give his daughter a special cursing for "letting that d—d nigger, Jo, have a pass." Hounds and hunters were at once called into requisition, but all in vain. All about the country was scoured and searched, but Uncle Ben's field was so public and he so honest, that no one thought of troubling it, or him.

Night came, and under cover of the first hour of darkness the two women were taken in charge by a man who led them rapidly along the railroad track till they came to a road where a carriage received them and they were driven rapidly into the city of Baltimore and there carefully secreted. Scarcely had they departed when a pack of hounds came into the field, and, after scenting around for some time, struck their track and were off in pursuit with such a wild scream as to waken the men from their quiet slumber.

Meanwhile the letter addressed to Mr. Jones was speeding on its way, and in due time on an editorial derived therefrom, the compositors in the office of the *Liberty Press* at Albany were busy, and on Friday Col. Hardy received a marked copy of that paper which informed him that his " chattels " arrived safe in Albany on Tuesday evening, and of course all farther effort for their recovery was stopped, though the atmosphere was for some time blue from the effects of the forcible vocabulary which this piece of news, manufactured specially for a southern market. eliminated from the old Colonel's tongue.

IV.

All iminent danger from direct pursuit being now over, early on Saturday evening Ben led the boys forth and placed them in charge of a sprightly colored boy about thirteen years of age, whom they were to keep constantly in sight as they passed through Baltimore, and, as he bestowed on them a little money, he said: " Now, boys, follah yer guide, and feah no danjah, and de good Lor' bress you and bring you safe to freedom."

With nimble steps they passed over the road to the city, and there stopped for a short time at a meeting of colored Methodists, of which faith were Jo and Harry, and joined lustily in the " Hallilujahs " and songs of praise. The meeting over, they fell in with the departing congregetion, and as they passed through the principal streets were veciforous in their praise of " the pow'fu' preachin' ob dat 'sidin' eldah, and de snipshus singin' ob de yaller gal wid de red rib'n," stopping occasionally to buy a few nuts or apples at some grocer's stand, ever keeping their little woolly headed conductor in sight, and before the hour forbidding the presence of colored people on the streets, were beyond the city limits, and again in company with Kate and Nancy, who had been brought to a place of rendezvous by a gentleman who proceeded to give the party specific instructions for the night. This done, fleetly they sped forward as directed until well towards day-dawn, when conductor Harry espied twc flickering lights placed side by side in an upper window, and exclaimed: "Bress de Lor' dah am de sign of rest."

"Yes, bress de Lor', O my sou'," ejaculated the thoroughly wearied Kate, "an if dis be de unner groun' railroad whar ebery one furnish his cah hisself, I'd radder ride wid ol' Lijah in a charyot ob fiah."

" Hush, honey, what foah you complain ? dis am gwine ober Jordan to de lan' ob res'."

"Yes, an' Jordan am a hard road to trabel, shu——" but the sentence was abruptly broken by the clear enunciation of "Thee will tarry here for the Sabbath."

The words proceeded from beneath a broad brimmed hat which emerged from among some shrubbery, and the party were quickly conducted into a spacious Quaker kitchen where a bountiful repast was in waiting for them, after partaking of which they were consigned to safe quarters for the day.

From this hospitable retreat, they sallied forth on Monday evening for another night journey, only to find in its ending a duplicate of the preceding one; and in this way the whole distance from Baltimore to Philadelphia was made on foot.

Once in the Quaker city, they were quietly put on a fishing smack and conveyed to Bordentown. At the latter place, under the management of a shrewd Quaker, a personal friend of the railroad agent, the boys were hid away among boxes and bales of goods in a freight car and were soon on their way to Gotham. Meanwhile the girls were dressed for the occasion, and at evening, closely veiled, just as the train was starting, were escorted into a coach by a gentleman assuming the full Southern air, and who had no hesitancy in pushing aside a watcher for runaways stationed at the door. At New York they again rejoined the "way freight," and the whole party were at once sent on to Albany, where they arrived after a journey of twenty days instead of two as supposed in Washington.

LAVINIA.

Apropos of the lamentable exhibitions of mob-violence, court-house burning, Sabbath desecration and election frauds presented by Cincinnati in the past few years, it may not be amiss to give a little exhibition of the spirit there manifested by the men of a past generation and see whence some of her present unenviable reputation comes. The city was well known to be intensely pro-slavery and to her came many a haughty Southron for purposes of business or pleasure, bringing with him more or less of his chattels as attendants. Among the comers of the summer of 1843, was a man named Scanlan, visiting his brother-in-law, one Hawkins. He brought with his family a pretty slave girl named Lavinia, some ten years old.

Before the party left New Orleans, the mother of the girl, a slave in that city, had given her the following admonitory instructian:—" Now 'Vinya, yer Massa's gwine for ter take yer Norf, an' wen yer gets to Sinsnate, chile, yer free, an' he'll sen' some good anj'l for to hide yer un'er him wing ; an' if you doan go wid him, but kum back to dis Souf wid yer ol' Massa, dis very han'll take yer black skin right off yer back shuah. Mebbe wen yer safe in dat free lan', yer ol' muder'll fin' yer thar if the good Lor' be willin '." Then she placed around the neck of the girl a small gold chain which was to be continually worn, that if they ever chanced to meet in Canada, the mother might know her child.

Once in Cincinnati, Lavinia began looking carefully for some "good anj'l," but instead, soon found two in the person of a colored man and his wife living near Mr. Hawkins'. To those she carefully committed her mother's counsel and threat. These parties entered heartily into her proposition to escape, and one night dressed her in a suit of boy's clothes and took her to the head of Spring street, near the foot of Sycamore Hill, and gave her in charge of Samuel Reynolds, a well-known Quaker, where she was successfully concealed for a number of days whilst Scanlan was raging about and as far as possible instituting a vigorous search.

Not far from Mr. Reynolds was the home of Edward Harwood in whose family resided John H. Coleman, a dealer in marble. The Harwoods and Colemans were ardent Abolitionists and ready to stand by any panting fugitive to the last. Mrs. Harwood's house stood on a side hill with a steep grade in front, and the narrow yard was reached by a flight of some twenty steps, whilst the side and rear were easily accessible.

After a time Mrs. Harwood, who had become much interested in Lavinia, took her home, where she was carefully concealed during the day, but allowed a little exercise in the dusk of the evening in the front yard, which was so high above the street as to be unobservable.

One evening when the girl was thus engaged the great house dog, Swamp, which always accompanied her kept up such a growling and snarling, as induced the men to think there might be foul play brewing and they went out several times but could detect nothing. Finally one of them said, "That child had better come in; some one may be watching for her," upon which Mrs. Coleman put her head out of the window and calling her by name, bade her come in, after which all was quiet for the night.

Dinner over the next day, the gentlemen had taken their departure down town, the ladies were busy about their work; an invalid gentleman was reclining in an easy chair and the girl had fallen asleep up-stairs, when a man suddenly appeared at the top of the flight of steps and very uncermoniously entered the front door which was open, and looking hurridly around roughly demanded, " Where's my child ? I want my child, and if you don't give her up there'll be trouble."

It needed no further evidence to convince the ladies it was Scanlan, an impression which had seized them both even before he had spoken, but then they were not the kind to be scared by his bluster, and Mrs. Coleman replied with spirit " You have no child here and if you were a gentleman you would not be here yourself."

At this Scanlon turned upon her and whilst his fists were clinched and his face livid with rage, exclaimed, " I tell you she is here, my slave girl,

JO NORTON. 31

Lavinia; I saw her last night myself; and if it had not been for you, madam, and that devlish dog there, I should have gotten her then. I had her nearly within my grasp when you bade her come in. I say where is my child? Give her up."

"You have no child here," coolly replied Mrs. Coleman again.

"I say I have, and if she hears me call she will answer me." Saying which he went to the stairway and called "Lavinia, Lavinia."

The child heard the voice, recognized it, and at once quietly hid herself within the bed. Though the call was repeated several times, no answer came, and Mrs. Coleman inquired, "Are you satisfied now?"

"I know my child is here, and you cursed Abolitionist have hidden her away," said the now almost frantic Scanlan. "You need not think you are going to fool me. I'm going to have my child, my slave, my property. I shall go down town and get a warrant and an officer to search your house, and you'll get no chance to run the girl away either, for I shall leave a guard over you whilst I am gone," then stepping to the door he said, "Hawkins, come in here," and the brother-in-law, before unseen by the inmates of the house, entered. "Now, Mr. Hawkins, I am going for a warrant, and I want you to see that my child does not get away till the officer comes," saying which Scanlon took his departure and Hawkins a seat, though evidently very ill at ease.

When part way down town the Southron recognized Mr. Harwood coming up the hill in his buggy, and thinking to intimidate him said, " I am after my slave girl who is in your house. Your women refuse to give her up. You will find the place well guarded, and I will soon have a warrant to search the place."

" I'll make it hotter than tophet for any one guarding my house, and the man who comes about my premises with a search warrant until I am accused of murder or theft, does so at his peril," was the warm reply, as Mr. Harwood started rapidly towards his home. Arriving there he thus addressed Mr. Hawkins: " I am told, sir, you are here to guard my house and family. We have need of no such attention, and if you do not immediately depart from our premises I shall pitch you headlong into the street. Be gone you miserable tool of a most miserable whelp." Just then the cowed and crest-fallen Hawkins made a practical application of his knowledge of Shakespeare, and stood not upon his going."

Remembering the great pro-slavery mob of 1836, when the office of James G. Birney's paper, *The Philanthropist*, was destroyed, and that of 1841, when but for the prompt action of Governor Corwin in aiding the arming of the students, an attack would have been made upon Lane Seminary as a "d—d Abolition hole," Scanlan hastened to the " Alhambra," then a popular saloon, gathered about him a band of roughs and after a treat all round proceeded to harangue them regarding his loss and also his unavailing efforts to regain his chattel. Under the influence of his speech and the more potent one of an open bar, the crowd readily promised him their support, and arranged to be at the hill in the evening time to see the fun.

Meantime Mr. Harwood was apprising his friends of the state of affairs, and these were beginning to gather at his house. One of them, an employee of Mr. Coleman, as he came up the hill, found a number of flags already set to guide the mob to the Harwood residence. These were torn down. Before the arrival of Mr. Coleman a crowd of excited people had assembled in the street below the house. Seeing among them an officer notorious for his cupidity and in entire sympathy with the slave catchers, Mr. Coleman approached him and shaking hands said, " Why how do you do, Mr. O'Neil? I am told you have a search-warrant for my house."

"For your house?"

" Yes ; here is where I live and I wish to know on what grounds you intend to search my house, as I am not aware of having laid myself liable to such a process."

" There must be some mistake," said the officer. "Indeed, Mr. Coleman, I must have been misinformed as to the merits of the case."

"Let me see the paper," persisted Mr. Coleman.

" No," said O'Neil, "there is a blunder somewhere,"

and he pushed his way, in a discomfited manner, through the crowd and disappeared.

As the crowd increased in the streets, the friends of Mr. Harwood arrived, until all the Abolitionists in the city, some forty in number, were present. Mr. Harwood stood on the front steps with Swamp, and when anyone evinced a purpose to ascend the steps the fine display of ivory in the dog's mouth cooled his ardor. Mr. Coleman and Alf. Burnet, afterwards well known in anti-slavery circles, went to a Dutch armory and secured a quantity of arms and ammunition; the women took up the carpet in the parlor which soon presented the appearance of a military bivouac, whilst papers and valuables were hurried off to other houses, and a strong guard was placed before the door. An application was made to the sheriff for protection, but he only replied, "If you make yourself obnoxious to your neighbors, you must suffer the consequences."

Whilst Scanlan was making his inflamatory speeches down town, and subsidizing the saloons, Lavinia was redressing in her boy's suit and was quietly taken out on a back street to a Mr. Emery's, the crowd meanwhile crying, "Bring out the lousy huzzy; where is the black b——ch?" and other equally classic expressions. One blear-eyed ruffian exclaimed, "If my property was in thar, I'd have it or I'd have the d—d Abolitionist's heart's blood, I would.' Another one, equally valorous called out, "Go in boys; why don't you go in?" and a score of

JO NORTON. 35

voices responded, " Go in yourself. The nigger ain't ourn. Where's the boss? Guess he's afraid of shootin' irons," a feeling that evidently pervaded the whole assemblage.

Being without a leader, and having no personal interest at stake, about dark the mob moved down the street, stoning and materially damaging the house of Alf. Burnett's father as they passed by. The old gentleman gathered up a large quantity of the missiles and kept them on exhibition for several years as samples of pro-slavery arguments.

Scanlan vented his spleen and breathed out his threatenings through the city papers, but being unable to get any redress, and finding he was to be prosecuted for trespass, he hastily decamped for New Orleans.

After a week or two, Livinia, dressed in her masculin suit went with some boys who were driving their cows to the hills to pasture, and was by them placed in the care of a *conductor*, by whom she was safely forwarded to Oberlin. Here she was found to have a fine mind, was befittingly educated, and ultimately sent as a missionary to Africa. After the lapse of several years she returned to this country, and whilst visiting the friends in Cincinnati, who had so kindly befriended her in the days of her childhood, suddenly sickened and died.

A RUSE.

Serious and earnest as was the work of our railroad, it was made the pretext for many a practical joke and arrant fraud. In the north part of Trumbull county, Ohio, lived an ancient agent named Bartlett, having in his employ a newly married man named DeWitt, a rollocking kind of a fellow, and well calculated to personate a son of Ham, or a daughter as well. DeWitt conspired with his wife and some of the female members of the old gentleman's family to have a little fun at Mr. Bartlett's expense. Some thrown off apparel of Mrs. Bartlett was procured from the garret, and, properly blackened, he was attired in a grotesque manner.

Just at evening a decrepid wench applied for admission at Mr. Bartlett's door. The women appeared very much frightened and were about shutting the door in her face, when the old gentleman, hearing the negro dialect came to the rescue. Soon the wanderer was comfortably seated, and to Mr. Bartlett's inquiry as to where she was from replied, "Oh Lor', Massa, I'se from ol' Virginny an' I'se boun' for Canady, and Massa Sutlifft, he tells me I mus' cum heah, but de white missus scare at dis ol' black face."

"O well, never mind that, they are all right now."

"Bress de Lor' for dat."

Speaking to his wife, Mr. Bartlett directed some supper be prepared before he should send her on.

"O no, Massa, I'se been done and eat supper dis bressed day.'

"Well, then, we'll arrange to send you on soon, but come and see my grandson," a lad lying sick in the other part of the room, saying which he arose and took the hand of the dame and led her to the bedside, and laying his hand across her stooped shoulders, began to speak tenderly of the little sufferer.

The risibilities of the counterfeit Dinah were now at their utmost tension and she contrived to place a foot heavily upon the caudal appendage of the great house dog lying near. There was a sudden bound of the brute, accompanied by a most unearthly howl, and away darted the decripit fugitive, shrieking, "O Lor' de houn', de houn'."

It was in vain the philanthropic old agent called after her, that there was no danger; on she sped until an opportunity offered to restore herself to Japhetic hue and male attire.

Mr. Bartlett long upbraided the female portion of his household for want of humanity on that occasion, but was allowed to die in blissful ignorance of the ruse played upon him, and DeWitt confessed that the ultimate fun derived therefrom scarcely compensated for the annoyance of the old gentleman and the trouble of removing the *cork*.

VI.

A year has passed anxiously at Albany with Jo. Rumors reached him that in an attempt to escape, Mary had been captured and sold into the south forever beyond his reach. Gathering up his earnings and bidding his companions good-by, he started rather aimlessly westward, and where he would have brought up no one can tell, had he not one day met a stranger, a pleasant, benevolent looking gentleman, near the village of Versailles, N. Y. It was just at the close of that most hilarious campaign in which the cry of " Tippecano and Tyler too," with " two dollars a day and roast beef," mollified with liberal potations of " hard cider," rendered " Little Matty Van a used up man," though the result was not yet ascertained, for no telegraph had learned to herald its lightning message in advance of time. If no other good came from the campaign, it had given every class of men the free use of the tongue in hurrahing for his favorite candidate, and foot-sore and hungry as he was, there was something about the gentleman that said to Jo, " Now is your opportunity," and touching his hat in genuine politeness he called out, " Hooraw for Ol' Tip."

Good naturedly the gentleman responded, " Well, my good fellow, it is a little late for you to be hurrahing for any candidate now that election is over, and, though you didn't quite strike my man, I shall find no fault. I know what you want more than 'hard cider.' It is a night's food and lodging."

" Thank you Massa, I'se tired and hungry, an' de fac' am I doan know what to do with myself."

"Well, no matter about that just now. Come along;" and Eber M. Pettit, long known as an earnest Abolitionist in Cattaraugus and Chautauqua counties, led the disheartened wanderer to his home, where, after supper, he questioned him as to his history, and when he had learned his unvarnished tale, he suggested that the man should stay with him that winter as a man-of-all-chores, and attend the village school.

As a result of that evening's conference there appeared among the children of the district school in a few days a colored man of about twenty five years of age, learning with the youngest of them his a b c. This was an innovation, unique in the extreme. Some of the villagers turned up their noses at the " nigger," but the social standing of Mr. Pettit, and the story of Jo which was freely circulated among the people, together with his genial disposition and kindness of manner, soon silenced all cavil and the school quietly progressed.

Learning that the editor of the *Liberty Press* was in Washington, Mr. Pettit addressed him in the following letter:

VERSAILLES, N. Y., Dec. 1, 1840.

Dear General.—I have at my house a colored man named Jo Norton. Something over a year ago he left a wife and child in the Capital, the property of a Mr. Judson. She was to have been brought off directly after he left, but the effort failed and he understands she has been sold South. Will you be so kind as to inquire into the matter aud see what can be done in the case if anything? Make your return to Jo Norton, direct.

Yours Truly,

E. M. PETTIT.

Gen. W. L. Chaplain,
    Washington, D. C.

This letter was duly posted, and on the morrow an ebony face, the very picture of expectancy, put in an appearance at the village post office with the query, "Any letter for Jo Norton, Massa pos' massa?" Thus it was twice a day for a week, when his unsophisticated importunity was rewarded by a missive bearing the address,

Jo Norton, Esq.,
Versailles,
Care E. M. Pettit, Esq.   *N. Y.*

and bearing the post-mark of the Capital. It read as follows:

Mr. Norton, *Dear Sir:*

The woman about whom Mr. Pettit wrote me is here. After her husband's escape she was detected in what was thought to be an effort to leave and was thrown into prison, where she lost an infant child. After three months she was visited by her master, and on a solemn promise never to make another effort to run away she was taken back to the family where she and the boy appear to be treated with great kindness. Though he has been offered $800 for her, Mr. Judson said he never sold a slave, and never will, but if her husband can raise $350 for them by March 4th, proximo, they will be given free papers so I can bring them North with me at that time.

Truly,

W. L. Chaplain.

At the reading of this letter, Jo, prompted by the fervent piety of his nature, broke into hysterical fits of laughter, interspersed with "Bress de Lor', bress de Lor'." But when the first paroxysm of joy was over he became very despondent, for he had no $350 and no friend to whom to appeal for it; but here, as before, Mr. Pettit came to the rescue.

"See here, Jo," he said, "there are nearly three months to the fourth of March, and yours is a wonderful story. You shall go forth and tell it to the people, and the money will come."

"Wy, bress de Lor', Massa Pettit, dis chile can nebber do dat. De people would jus' laf at de nigger."

"Never mind the laugh, Jo. If you love Mary and the boy you can stand the laughing. Now be a man. I will go with you and see you start;" and before bed-time he had laid out the work for his ward, in whom he had now become thoroughly interested, and had listened several times to his rehearsal of his story of escape and tale of plantation life, and offered such suggestions as he thought advisable, and that night Jo went to bed " to sleep; to dream." To dream of wife and boy in slavery, and himself making speeches among the white people of the North for their deliverance.

The next morning Mr. Pettit went out into the country a few miles where he had a number of Abolition friends and made full arrangements for Jo's speaking there early the next week. In the meantime the word was thoroughly circulated whilst Jo was most effectively schooled to his new field, and on the appointed evening the school-house was filled to overflowing. Jo told his story in such a manner as to draw out rounds of approbative applause from the mouths of the audience, and six dollars from their pockets when the hat was passed round. Meetings were held immediately in the several school districts in the vicinity with marked success, and then Jo, highly inspired, left school and started out on a systematic course of lectures which took him to Westfield, Mayville and other villages of Chautauqua county as well as Cattaraugus.

On the 25th day of January Mr. Pettit received the following from Washington:

"*Dear Pettit.*—If Judson can have $300 by February first, he will deliver up the woman and child of whom we have had correspondence.
In haste,
W. L. CHAPLAIN."

He hastened to Ellicottville and found that Jo had already realized $100. A meeting was immediately called in an office in the village, at which were present Judge Chamberlin, of Randolph, E. S. Coleman, of Dunkirk, and several other gentlemen. The letter was read, and at the suggestion of the Judge a note for two hundred dollars was drawn and signed by ten of them, with the understanding that they were to share equally in the payment of any deficit after Jo had done his best. The money was advanced by Mr. Coleman, and one of the party drove fifty miles to Buffalo, through a pelting storm, purchased a draft, forwarded it to Mr. Coleman, and before the "days of grace" had expired Mary and her child were duly registered and delivered as free people.

Meanwhile Jo's story had gotten into the papers of Western New York, and he had calls from various places to lecture; indeed, he had become quite a local lion, and so successful that early in March when word came that Mary and the child had reached Utica, he was the possesser of $195. This he deposited in the hands of Mr. Pettit who returned him $30 and told him to go and make provision for his wife and child, and pay the balance of the note when he could. Though he had walked that day from Buffalo, a distance of nearly thirty miles, Jo immediately returned, and early the next day, in the home of a leading Abolitionist in Utica there was a regular " Hal'lujer; Bress de Lor', for de Lor' will bress his people," time when Jo and Mary met after their seemingly hopeless separation.

VII.

Ten years and more had passed; the Ellicottville note had been long settled; Jo had laid aside his mission as a lecturer and gone into business in Syracuse, N. Y., where he owned a pleasant home and had a family of intelligent children attending the public school; New York State, like the country at large, had been convulsed over the slavery question, and the city of his adoption had become a town of intensely Abolition sentiment. As the outgrowth of the slavery agitation there had come the enactment of the "Fugitive Slave Law," as it was popularly, or rather unpopularly called, by means of which the

South thought to render imperative the rendition of their runaway slaves. But they had counted without their host. Though successful in cracking their whips over the heads of Northern law-makers in the Capitol, the great mass of the people of the free states, no matter what their political affiliations, felt outraged at the idea of being converted into a set of legally constituted slave hunters. Few places more excited the ire of the chivalry than Syracuse, and the threat was defiantly made that if another anti-slavery convention was held in the city it should be enlivened by the seizure of a fugitive of whom a test case could be made.

Not to be thus intimidated, a call for such a convention was issued and at the appointed time commenced. Whilst the delegates were organizing in the old Market Hall, in a cooper shop in another part of the city, all unconscious of danger, a colored man named Jerry, who had some years before escaped from slavery, was busy engaged at his labor, when he was suddenly pounced upon by a marshal and his deputies from Rochester, and, after a brave resistance, overpowered, manacled and thrown into a cart secured for that purpose, and hurried away to the commissioner's office, closely guarded. The news of the arrest spead like wild-fire, and soon the streets were thronged with excited people. A man rushed into the convention and called out: "Mr. President a fugitive has been arrested and they are trying to hurry him away." Without motion, the convention adjourned, and the delegates and attendants were added to the throng already in the street. The uproar was equal to that, when, for the "space of two hours," the people cried, "Great is Diana of the Ephesians," but more concentrated, and the cause of coming together better understood.

Jerry was hurried into the commissioner's office, the lower door to which was heavily barred and the upper one securely bolted, so that it was with difficulty that his council and more immediate friends obtained admission.

The court once opened, within there was contention, parley, quibble and delay until twilight fell; without, the building was immediately surrounded by fugitives who had found an asylum in and about the city, and free colored people, among whom Jo Norton towered like Saul among his brethren, and beyond these an immense multitude of citizens who had stood waiting all the afternoon of that eventful day, manifesting no disposition to retire.

When it was announced that the court had adjourned for supper, it was soon evident that the decisive hour had come. A heavy timber was lifted to the shoulders of some sturdy negroes, and using the temporary space accorded them, at the watchword "Jo" they hurled it with such force against the door that bars and hinges gave way, and Norton, crowbar in hand, at the head of a storming column entered the stairway hall. The marshal was a man of nerve and disclaimed against any attempt on the inner door, but in vain. A few vigorous blows of the crowbar forced it open; there was the sharp report of a pistol succeeded by a quick blow of the bar, and Jo unharmed, stood master of the situation, whilst the right arm of the marshal hung useless at his side. The posse scattered, the marshal saving himself by jumping from the second story window and skulking away in the dark; Jerry, who had been very roughly treated, was unloosed, and by daylight was well on his way to Canada, whilst the convention resumed its deliberations the next day amid the congratulations of many who before had looked upon its purpose with indifference or absolute opposition.

As for Jo, though defying slave-hunters and their hirelings as such, having now arrayed himself by an act of violence against the government, he took the advice of judicious friends, and soon removed to Canada, where for years he was an esteemed citizen, and a friend and adviser of those who came to his locality as fugitives.

VIII.

As an index of Jo's native quickness of perception, the following excerpts, taken from Pettit's "Sketches of the Underground Railroad," published some years ago by W. McKinstry & Son, are added, the only change being that the places where the events are thought to have taken place are given.

"Jo was a serious, devoted Christian, yet his wit

JO NORTON.

and mirthfulness were often exhibited in keen, sarcastic repartee. At Delanti the question was asked, 'Did you work hard when you were a slave?'

'No! I didn't work hard when I could help it.'

'Did you have enough to eat?'

'Yes, such as it was.'

'Did you have decent clothes?'

'Yes, midlin'.'

'Well, you were better off than most people are here, and you were a fool to run away.'

'Well, now, the place I lef' is there yet, I s'pose. Guess nobody's never got into it, and if my frien' here wants it, he can have it fo' the askin,' though p'raps he better get his *member of Congress to recommend him.*'"

"At Westfield, a fellow asked, 'Is the speaker in favor of amalgamation?'

''Gamation! what's dat?'

'It means whites and blacks marrying together.'

'O dat's it! as fo' such things they 'pends mostly on peples' tas'. Fo' my part, I have a colored woman fo' a wife,—that's my choice,—an' if my frien' here wants a black wife, an' if she is pleased with him, I'm suah I shant get mad about it.'"

"Soon after he commenced collecting funds to redeem his family from bondage, he was invited to go to a school house in Villenova. When near the place he saw two boys chopping, and heard one of them say: 'There's the nigger.'

"Jo stopped and said: 'I ain't a nigger! I

allus pays my debts; my massa was a *nigger*. See here! when you chop, you be a chopper, ain't dat so?'

'Yes,' responded the boys.

'Well, when a man *nigs*, I call him a *nigger*. Now ol' massa nigged me out of all I earned in my life. Of course he is a nigger.' Then Jo sang the chorus to one of Geo. W. Clark's Liberty songs:

> 'They worked me all de day,
> Widout one cent of pay;
> So I took my flight
> In de middle ob de night,
> When de moon am gone away.'

'Now, boys, come over to the school-house this evening and I'll sing you the res' of it.' That evening Jo had a full house and a good collection."

THE ORIGINAL "JERRY."

Having given a brief account of the "Jerry Rescue" at Syracuse, a circumstance fraught with momentus consequences, and no inconsiderable factor in precipitating the "Impending Crisis," I now pass to consider the real original "Jerry Rescue."

In the early summer of 1834, there came to Austinburg, Ohio, a colored man of middle age, of whose escape to Ohio tradition, even, gives little account, only that he was the property of a Baptist deacon who followed him in close pursuit. Both parties upon the ground, matters became marvellously lively in the quiet country town.

JO NORTON. 49

Jerry was shifted from place to place, but the deacon would in some way get a clue to his whereabouts, and another move would be made to thwart the pursuer, some one being always ready to ask him what he would take for the man; but it was always with him, " I want the nigger, not money."

Wearied at length with the continued baffling, and believing he had found the retreat of his chattel, the pious deacon went to Jefferson and secured the service of Sheriff Loomis to make an arrest. The twain came upon him just before day-break, but not to catch him napping. He was up and off just in time to elude their grasp but not until they caught a glimpse of him making across the fields in the direction of Eliphalet Austin's, who lived near where Grand River Institute now stands.

Rapping at the door, Jerry was admitted by Mr. Austin, who was just in the act of dressing himself. Reading in the excited manner of the fugitive the state of the case, Mr. Austin pointed under the family bed where his wife still lay. Jerry took the hint, and in a moment was hugging the wall in the darkest corner under the bed. Mr. Austin quietly closed the bed-room door, started a fire, and was at the well drawing a pail of water when the pursuers came up.

" Have you seen my nigger this morning? " queried the Deacon.

"It is pretty early to see an object so dark as a colored man, if that is what you are inquiring about," was the response.

"Well, early as it is, we have seen him, and believe he is secreted in your house."

"Oh, you do, do you? Well, gentlemen, you have the fullest liberty to search my premises and satisfy yourselves," and, whilst the sheriff kept watch without, Mr. Austin furnished the Southerner the most abundant opportunity within. Candle in hand he led the way to the cellar, then to the garret. The children's bed-rooms and the closets of the chamber, the parlor, spare bed-room and pantry below were all carefully examined, but no Jerry was found, and the Deacon apologetically remarked: "I beg your pardon, Mr. Austin, for this intrusion, and for the injustice I did you in supposing you were harboring my slave."

"What," said Mr. Austin, who was also a pious man and a licentiate minister, I hope you are not through looking yet."

"Why, I have been all over the house already."

"O no, you have not been in my wife's bed-room yet," said he rather sarcastically. "Go in, Deacon. Wife is not up yet; you may find your 'nigger' with her."

Dropping his head in very shame, the Deacon excused himself, and going out, with the sheriff rode off.

As soon as they were well out of sight, Jerry was taken to the woods and hidden in an old sugar house, where he remained for some days. Meanwhile time and perplexity began to soften the Deacon, and he finally concluded that three hundred and fifty dollars ($350) in hand would be worth more than " a nigger on foot," which was raised and paid over, the original subscription being now in the hands of the writer.

The money paid over and the freedom papers made out, the Deacon had no difficulty in obtaining an interview with Jerry, a meeting very satisfactory to the latter personage, now that he could meet " Ol' Massa on perfec' 'quality as gemen."

There were two things connected with this case which the sturdy old Austinburgers always regretted. The one was that as the work of purchase was completed late Saturday afternoon, the Deacon accepted the proffered hospitality of Mr. Austin for the Sabbath, and with him attended church in the old historic "meeting house" at the Center, where the Rev. Henry Cowles dispensed the gospel in the form of a red-hot anti-slavery sermon, to which the Deacon listened with great expressed satisfaction if not profit. During the evening service, some unprincipaled persons shaved his horse's main and tail, which, when known, led several of the first citizens of the town to save its reputation and show their appreciation of the gentlemanly qualities of their visitor, by giving him in exchange for his disfigured horse one equally good, thus sending him back to Dixie with a high regard for their honesty, as well as sincerity.

The other was, Jerry, once a free man, went to Conneaut and established himself as a barber, but unable to bear prosperity, he soon fell into habits of drinking and dissipation, thus rendering worthless the investment philanthropy and generosity had made in him.

The following is the subscription referred to above, together with the names of donors and the amount given so far as they can be deciphered:

We whose names are hereto affixed, promise to pay to Eliphalet Austin the sums put to our names, for the purpose of liberating from slavery a colored man whose master is supposed to be in pursuit, and offers to free him for three hundred and fifty dollars.

Austinburg, July 23, 1834.

Eliphalet & Aaron E Austin. $50.
J. Austin, $40.00.
J. S. Mills, $2.00.
A. A. Barr, $1.00.
G. W. St. John, $25.00.
Luman Whiting, $2.00.
I. Hendry, $5.00.
Amos Fisk, $5.00.
Daniel Hubbard, $1.00.
Mr. Sawtell, $2.00.
L. M. Austin, $5.00.
Dr. A. Hawley, $2.00.
Ward, $5.00.
Jefferson, $20.00.

Orestes K. Hawley, $50.
L. Bissell, $20.00.
T. H. Wells, $3.00.
Harvey Ladd, Jr., $2.00.
James Sillak, $3.00.
Benjamin Whiting, $1.00.
Giddings & Wade, $10.
Russell Clark, $2.00.
Henry Harris, $1.00.
E. Austin, Jr., $15.00.
Ros. Austin, $5.00.
W. Webb, Jr., $5.00.
Henry, $5.00.
A Friend, 50 cents.

The $20.00 from Jefferson was a kind of *religious* collection.

A COOL WOMAN.

Apropos the deliberation of Mr. Austin, there comes an incident from southern Ohio illustrating how cool a woman may be in case of emergency. A slave named Zach had escaped from Virginia and was resting and recuperating himself in the family of a benevolent man in one of the southern counties previously to pursuing his onward course, when one evening the house was surrounded by his owner and a number of other men, and the right of searching the premises demanded. The husband was much agitated and appealed to his wife to know what was to be done.

"Why," said she, "let them in, and search the lower part of the house first, and leave Zack to me."

"But I tell you, wife, the man can't be got off without being caught."

"Don't I know that? Do as I say."

The husband took her advice, and whilst he was leading a searching party through the cellar and lower rooms of the house, she placed the fugitive carefully between the feather and straw ticks of the family bed, and by the time the posse reached the room she was composedly in bed as though nothing unusual was transpiring. The result was that the search proved a bootless one, and the whole party left, believing they had been misdirected by some one bent on deceiving them.

CHAPTER II.

JACK WATSON.

FIFTY years ago there lived in Caldwell County, Kentucky, a well-to-do individual named Wilson. He owned a large estate, to which was attached numerous slaves. Such was the character of the master that bondage sat lightly upon them. Provident and indulgent, Mr. Wilson allowed his people to do largely as they chose. To them the words of the old plantation song,

"Hang up de shubel and de hoe."

had much of reality.

Strangers came and went among them freely; they heard much of the ways of escape northward, of which many from plantations surrounding them availed themselves, but the bonds of affection were so strong between Mr. Wilson and his people that no effort was ever made on the part of the latter to escape. But things were not always to remain thus. In 1853, Mr. Wilson sickened and died, a circumstance which brought not only grief but consternation to his "people," for they soon learned they were to be divided among the heirs. Jack and Nannie, a brother and sister who had grown up on the estate tenderly attached to each other and to their old

A SLAVE HUNT.

JACK WATSON.

master, fell to the lot of a drunken and licentious man named Watson, who took them to his farm in Davies County, not far from the Ohio River. Here, as common field hands, they were brutally treated, and soon began to plan means of escape. Before these were consummated the old cook died, and Nannie, who was of attractive form and manners, was taken from the field to fill her place. This only added to the degradation of her condition, for she was now continually called upon to repel the lecherous advances of her brutal master. As a punishment for this she was at length placed in close confinement from which her brother succeeded in freeing her. They set out at once for the river, hoping to escape, but were soon overtaken, brought back and so cruelly whipped by Watson, that Nannie soon died from the effects.

The sight of his lacerated, dying sister, the only tie that bound him to earth, continually haunted Jack, and he vowed escape, and vengeance if it were possible. His plans were carefully laid. In perambulating the numerous swamps in the neighborhood whose outlets led to the river, he had discovered a hollow tree broken off some twenty feet above the surrounding water. By climbing an adjacent sappling he discovered that the hollow within the stub would furnish a secure and comfortable retreat, should necessity require. By divers acts of plantation civility he had gained the confidence of "Uncle Jake" and "Aunt Mary," an old couple who sympathized deeply with him, and promised him any aid in their power, provided it was such as "Massa'll neber know." All Jack asked was that in case he disappeared, they should set the third night after his disappearance something to eat on a shelf where he could reach it, and every fourth night thereafter until it should, for two successive times, be untaken. He also gave them in keeping a package of cayenne pepper to be placed with the edibles. In his visits to the river he had noted the fastenings of the skiffs, and had provided himself with both a file and an iron bar which would serve the double purpose as a means of defense and for drawing a staple. These he carefully secreted in his prospective retreat, waiting only an opportunity to occupy it.

Such an opportunity was not long in presenting itself, for one night the master came home late from a drunken revel, and found Jack awaiting him as ordered. Becoming enraged at some supposed act of disobedience, he flew at Jack with an open knife. The hour of vengeance had come. Seizing a hoe, with a single stroke Jack felled him to the ground, a lifeless form. A moment only he waited to view the gaping wound—to compare it with poor Nan—then gathering up a few things that he could, he was off with the fleetness of a deer. Passing two or three miles down the country, he entered the outlet of the swamp, and after passing down it for some distance, keeping so near the shore as to make his tracks observable, he struck in, directly reversing his footsteps, and before the dawn was safely ensconsed in his selected tower.

Morning came and with it the knowledge of Watson's death. The cause was easily divined—there was the bloody hoe, and Jack, who was left to wait his coming, was gone. Blood hounds and fierce men were soon upon his trail. His course was easily traced to the brook, and his descending footsteps discerned, but no trace of him could be discovered beyond that. The greater part thought he had reached the river, and escaped to the Indiana shore by swimming, at which he was an expert, or had been drowned in the attempt. Others believed his footsteps only a decoy and searched all the adjacent swamps, sometimes passing very near him, but all in vain. Flaming posters, advertising him, were sent broadcast, and slave-catchers on both sides of the river were on the alert.

On the second day a great concourse assembled at Watson's funeral. There were many conjectures, and much argument, and loud swearing about the "nigger" who had done the deed, and as a means of intimidating the weeping—none mcre so than Uncle Jake and Aunt Mary—chattels gathered around, terrible things were promised Jack should he be caught.

The services over, the crowd dispersed, and the next morning all hands were set to work as usual. At night when all was quiet, Aunt Mary, whose cabin was the farthest of any from the "mansion," placed a liberal ration of hoe cake and bacon, together with the pepper, upon the designated shelf, and betook herself to the side of Uncle Jake who was already resting his weary limbs in the land of forgetfulness. Shortly after midnight a hand was thrust cautiously through the open window, the packages were softly lifted, a little pepper was deftly sifted in retreating footsteps, and in a short time Jack was safe again in his water-shut abode, and when old uncle and auntie were talking of the "wun'ful ang'l" that had visited the house that night, Jack was quietly enjoying a morning nap.

Several weeks passed, the excitement about Watson had measurably died away, two successive depositions of provisions had been left untouched and the good old couple knew "Dat de angel was feedin' Jack no moa', like de rabens fed ol' 'Lijer." They were sure, " Jack am safe."

Taking his appliances, Jack had descended the outlet some distance one starlight night, and then striking across the country, had reached the river just below the little village he had been accustomed to visit before the death of his sister. The finding of a skiff and the wrenching away of the fastening occupied but a short time and at daylight he was safely secreted in an Indiana forest. Knowledge previously gained enabled him soon to put himself in charge of an underground official, but instead of making direct for Canada he shipped for the Quaker settlement near Salem, Ohio, of which he had heard

JACK WATSON.

much from a fruit tree dealer before the death of Mr. Wilson, and ultimately, in the quaint home of Edward Bonsall found a secure asylum, and in his nurseries desirable employment, so far from his former home that little disturbed his mind except the frequent recurring remembrances of his slain master with the cruelly lacerated form of his sister ever rising in justification of the summary punishment that had been inflicted upon him.

II.

In the autumn of 1856, Jack went with Mr. Bonsall to Pittsburgh. Whilst walking along the street, he met face to face a half-brother of his late master. At first sight he thought it an apparition and turned and ran rapidly away, but not until he was himself recognized. So dextrous had been his motions that he eluded the pursuit immediately instituted and was soon among the hills beyond the city limits.

Hand bills minutely describing him were again widely circulated, particularly along the belt of country bordering the Pittsburgh and Erie canal, as it was argued he would try and make his escape by that route to Canada, and all the appliances of an odious law were called into requisition to secure his apprehension.

III.

Rap, rap, rap, came a knuckle against the door of Thomas Douglass, of Warren, Ohio, in the silent hours of the night. Such occurrences were not frequent of late at the home of the honest Englishman whose love of justice and humanity had risen above all fear of the pains and penalties of an unrighteous law. Hastily dressing himself, he inquired, "Who comes?"

"Ol' Diligence," a name recognized at once by Mr. Douglass as the appelation of a colored conductor from Youngstown.

"Hall right; wat's aboard?"

"Subjec', Massa Douglass, and hard pressed, too."

"'Ard pressed his 'e? Well, come in."

The door was opened, a brief explanation followed, and Jack Watson and "Old Diligence" were consigned to a good bed for the night. In the morning his faithful guide, who had himself escaped from bondage many years before gave Jack some money, a supply of which he always had in hand, and left him with the emphatic assurance, "Massa Douglass am a true man." But Jack was hard to be assured, and when seated at breakfast with the master machinist's hands, he trembled like an aspen.

Three gentlemen, Levi Sutliff, John Hutchins and John M. Stull had been early summoned to devise the best means for forwarding Jack safely. The two former of these had been long experienced operators; the latter was rather a novice at the business. A few years previously, an ambitious young man, he had gone south as a teacher, thinking little and caring less about the "peculiar institution." He had been

JACK WATSON. 61

in Kentucky but a short time when a slave auction was advertised and his Buckeye inquisitiveness prompted him to witness it. Two or three children were struck off and then the mother, a well formed, good-looking octaroon, was put upon the block.

"Now, gentlemen," said the auctioneer, a hard-shelled Baptist preacher, "I offer you a valuable piece of property. She's a good cook; can make clothes, or handle a hoe as well as a man. She's a healthy woman, gentlemen, an more'n that, she's a Christian. Gentlemen, she's a member of my own congregation."

The buyers crowded around. They examined her teeth, her hands, her feet, her limbs as though she had been a horse on sale.

Our spectator began to feel himself getting white in the face, and swear words were rising in his throat, and he beat a hasty retreat.—John was under conviction.

A few mornings after our young teacher was wakened by the sound of heavy blows and cries of pain proceeding from another part of the hotel. That evening when Harry, the boy appointed his special waiter, came to his room, Mr. Stull cautiously inquired who had been punished in the morning.

"Dat was me Massa. De ol' boss gib'd me a buckin."

"What was the trouble, Harry, and what is a bucking?"

"Why Lor' bress you, Massa, dis chile slep' jus' a

minit too long, an' de ol' boss cum'd wid his 'buck,' a board wid a short han'l and full ob holes, an' he bent Harry ober, like for to spank a chil', an' o Lor' how he struck." (Then lowering his voice,) "Say, Massa Stull, can you tell de Norf star?"

The boy had been all care, attention and manliness. The soul of the teacher was fully aroused.— Stull was converted.

Waiting the coming of these gentlemen, Jack had gone into the back yard, and when they arrived he was nowhere to be found. A prolonged search failed to reveal his whereabouts, and when at length night fell kind Mrs. Douglass placed an ample plate of provisions in the back kitchen and continued it for several weeks, hoping he might return, but no *angel* ever spirited a particle of it away.

IV.

Years ago, even before Wendell Phillips, Abbey Kelley and others of their school began to hurl their bitter anathemas at the institution of slavery, there lived upon a far-reaching Virginia plantation in the valley of the James a man who had taken a truly comprehensive and patriotic view of the institution that was blighting the reputation of his state, as well as impoverishing her soil. He had inherited his fine estate, encumbered by a large number of slaves, and his soul revolted at the idea of holding them in bondage. A man of fine physique, commanding mien and superior intellectual endowments, John

JACK WATSON.

Young could not brook the idea of eating bread that savored of the sweat of another's brow, and the thought of living amid the withering, blighting scenes of slave labor and slave traffic was not at all congenial to his tastes. Casting about, he soon found a purchaser for his broad acres. Before disposing of his plantation, however, he made a trip into western Pennsylvania, and in Mercer county, on the rich bottoms of Indian run, made purchase of an extensive tract of valuable land. Returning to the Old Diminion, he at once concluded the sale of his estate, and vowed his intention of going North.

His friends were amazed at the idea of his becoming a "Pennymite" farmer, and his people were thrown into consternation, as they expected soon to be exposed on the auction block. The sallies of one class he easily parried; the fear of the other he quickly allayed by calling them together and presenting them with freedom papers. There was a moment of silence, of blank astonishment, and then arose shouts, and cries, and hallelujahs to God, amid laughter and tears, for this wonderful deliverance.

When the excitement had somewhat subsided the late master revealed to them the fact that he was going north where it was respectable for a white man to labor, and if any of them should ever come his way they would see him chopping his own wood and hoeing his own corn, and that they were now free to go where they chose, only they must see they did not lose their papers.

"Bress de good Lor', Massa, we'll go wid you to dat new plantashun and be spect'ble too, and make light work for ol' Massa."

Though foreign to the purpose of Mr. Young, he yielded to the importunity of those he had manumitted, and soon there appeared on the Pennsylvania purchase a spacious residence, built rather in the Virginia style, and around it were grouped numerous cabins, occupied by the sable colony that had followed the Caucassian proprietor. The family equipage was brought along, and Alexander Johnson always persisted in being Massa's coachman and driving him in state.

The farm improved rapidty under the guidance of intelligence, aided by paid labor, and John Young's house soon became known as a hospitable home, and to none more so than to the fugitive from bondage, for he early became an influential agent on the great thoroughfare to Canada.

Securing the aid of a few neighbors and friends, rather as a matter of compliment than otherwise, Mr. Young had erected, at a convenient site, a nice country chapel, now a Methodist church in which the writer has been privileged to speak, and here the people of the neighborhood, white and black, met for worship.

The Sabbath evening service in this little church had closed and the speaker, J. W. Loguen, an eloquent man, though a former fugitive from slavery, but at that time pastor of a Baptist church in Syracuse, N. Y., and largely engaged in the underground transit business, sat conversing with Mr. Young, in the home of the latter gentleman, when Uncle 'Lec, as the old coachman was familiarly called, entered and excitedly exclaimed, " Mass Young, him am come, him am come."

" Who has come, Alec?" queried the host kindly.

" Wh, Massa, dat runaway wot de han' vill tell bout, an' him am fearfu' scar' an' no mistake, fo' he say de catchers am arter him shua."

"Bring him in, Alec," said Mr. Young, and in a moment more there was ushered into the room a tall, muscular colored man, bearing evident traces of white blood and answering fully the description of Jack Watson. His story, other than what we have already learned, was that at Warren, being suspicious of so many white men, he had gone out of the back yard of Mr. Douglass and a short distance along the canal and secreted himself until night in an old ware-house, still well remembered as bearing the inscription, " Forwarding and Commission. M. B. Taylor & Co." In the evening he had struck out for Indian Run, of which Old Diligence had told him. He had traveled all the night, but not being able to reach his destination, had lain secreted during the day, and now hungry and fearful he appealed to Mr. Young for food and protection, both of which were readily accorded.

After the cravings of appetite had been satisfied, a conference was held, and it was decided that Jack should try and make Syracuse, after which Mr.

Loguen would assure both safety and employment. Owing to the well-known character of Mr. Young and his attaches, and unmistakable evidences of close pursuit that had preceded Jack's coming, it was further determined to forward him at once to "Safe Haven." In accordance with this decision the family carriage, an imposing piece of "rolling stock," soon stood at the door with 'Lec consequentially seated upon the box. A moment later, Jack, Mr. Loguen, and stalwart John Young emerged from the mansion, and as they took their seats in the carriage, Mr. Young said: "Now, Alec, look well to your lines and remember the 'Haven' is to be made before daylight."

"Yes, Massa, dis ol' chile keep an eye to de lines, de road, an' anyting 'spicuous, an' rouse up ol' missus long afor' de chicken' 'gin to crow," saying which, he gave a gentle chirrup and the carriage went rolling away to the northward.

V.

Whoever was accustomed, a third of a century ago, to travel over the road from Warren, O., to Meadville, Pa., will remember a wayside inn, whose sign bore in German character the euphonious name of "Aughfeultwangher House." The house itself, like its name, was of German origin, a genuine example of a Dutch farm house, bespeaking both comfort and thrift. The occupants were of the same name as the house, the proprietor being an honest, quiet, well-meaning man, with no special personality. Not so his better half, however. She was a character —a decided personality. Kind and generous, she had a temper, which when let loose became a very tornado. She was neat and tidy as a housekeeper, and unexcelled as a cook. A regular embodiment of piety and profanity; of sympathy and execration; of wit, repartee and scurrilous invective, her very off-handedness made the house immensely popular with drovers and road-men, and it was quoted from the prairies of the west to the Quaker City itself; and many is the man who has traveled an extra five miles to gain the hospitable roof of the "Awful-tricker House," as it came to be called by those who failed to accomplish the German of it.

As an illustration of the without and the within of the place, a little personal experience is introduced. At the end of a bleak November day, I found myself taking the advice of a friend and making an extra exertion with jaded beast, in order to enjoy the hospitality of the "Aughfeultwangher." Knowing the reputation of the hostess I greeted her with: "Well, Auntie, can you keep a stranger to-night?"

Looking at me with a quizical expression and evidently pleased at the appellation used, she replied: "Dot is von long face to keeps all in von house."

"O, well, never mind, I can let a part of it stay in the barn."

"Vell, I guess we growds es all in dem house," and running to the back door, she called out, "Fater, fater, here bist einer mann, unt ein pferd vas Shineral Shackson rote. Nehms du es dem stolle vilst Ich das abend essen for dem manne erhalten."

Obedient to the summons the host came at once, and took the wearied beast, whilst I was ushered into the little bar-room, whose well-filled box-stove was sending out a genial warmth, and away went the sprightly dame to prepare supper, whose savory odors soon filled the house.

Directly the door into the great family kitchen opened, and I did not wait for a repitition of the hearty "Coome Meister, your supper bist ready." Entering, I found the room seated after the German style, and was greeted with the sight of a great, open fire-place, with its bake-oven and pot-hole attachment. Upon the table were rich slices of ham, eggs, bread, such as only a genuine German woman can bake, and other things in abundance. When I was seated and the good woman had poured out a cup of delicious coffee, she took a chair opposite, and after eying me a moment, inquired:

"Vell, Meister, var from you come?"

"From Ohio, auntie."

"You bist von Yankee, then."

"No, I'm a Buckeye."

"Von Puckeye! vas ish dat, eh?"

"One born in Ohio."

"Unt vas your fater ein Sherman?"

"No, auntie, but my grandfather was."

"O your grossfater. Vell, I tot dare vas some Shermeny blud; dot lickt hair und blau eyes zint der sign, meister."

"Well, auntie, 'tis not bad blood, is it."

"O nein. Mein Got, es ist dot best, but das Yankee is shust so goot," to which of course I assented, with the remark that the two together are a little better, thus causing the old lady to laugh outright.

After a moment's pause, in which there seemed to be a studying of what tactics to pursue, she said, "Vell, meister, it bist none of my pisness, but vas you stoon in das velt?"

Wishing to make a fine conquest, I summoned what little German I could muster and replied, "Ich bin einer school-meister."

"Got in himmel! du bist einer schulmeister, O Ich vish de kinder vare to house—"

Just then the host came in, and there was a rapid discharge of pure German between them, the outcome of which was a passing of a very pleasant evening, though the English on the one side and the German on the other were both very broken, and when the hour for retiring came I was escorted by the old couple to what was evidently the best room in the house. Approaching the bed the hostess laid back a fine feather tick, revealing sheets of snowy whiteness overspreading another, and then with a feeling of conscious pride exclaimed, "Dot, Her Schulmeister, is mine bester bett, unt do canst schlafen on der top, in der mittel or unter das bett, shust as you bleze. Guten abent."

Such was the house, such were the Aughfeultwanghers, with the addition of being Jacksonian Democrats of the straightest sect, the least likely people, apparently, to have any sympathy with the underground work, yet shrewd John Young, ever fertile in expedients, had approached this couple, and as a result of the conference there was arranged a snug little room over and back of the oven with the way of entry by the pot-hole. This room was never to be occupied but by one individual, and he was to be brought by Mr. Young in person, who was also to provide for the taking away. In view of these facts he had christened the place "Safe Haven," and its existence, outside of the family, was known only to himself, Alec and one or two others of his retainers and "Mose" Bishop, a tall, slim man, residing at Linesville, having a perfect hatred of creeds and cant, but an enthusiastic supporter of every cause demanding sympathy and justice, and who on account of his Jehu style of driving, was known along the *road* as "The Lightning Conductor."

VI.

True to his promise, before the first cock had sounded the approaching morn on that late October night, Alec reined up at the Aughfeultwangher, and Mr. Young, alighting, rapped at the door, and all questions being satisfactorily answered, Jack was admitted, and the carriage rolled rapidly down to the little village at the foot of Conneaut lake, and at the hotel breakfast was ordered for men and beasts.

Having washed themselves, they were waiting the progress of culinary processes in the kitchen, meanwhile regailing themselves by reading the hand-bill advertising Jack, which was conspicuously posted in the bar-room, when two horsemen, one a constable from Mercer county, rode up and also ordered breakfast and feed for their horses.

The constable and Mr. Young readily recognized each other, and though no word was pased it was evident to each that his business was understood by his neighbor, hence the breakfast passed in silence, and when his bill was settled, the carriage of the ex-Virginian took a homeward direction.

No sooner was it gone than the constable remarked to Boniface, "I have been after that turnout all night. When it started there was a *passenger* in it, answering to that bill there."

"You've been making the old fellow a close call," said the landlord, "but you'll find him a hard one to handle."

Yes; but if I could catch the nigger, the $500 wouldn't come bad. We have been close on his track for several days. We know he was at Young's last night but where in the d—— he is now is the question."

"Dropped somewhere, likely."

"Yes, *dropped*. Old Alec was too much for us, and we lost the trail. From which direction did they come?"

"From towards Meadville."

"Do you know any station that he could have touched?"

"No, unless Aughfeultwaugher's."

"Awfultricker's! ha! ha! Upon my life that is a bright idea. Why the old woman would make even Young think the day of judgment had come if he were to bring a nigger to her home."

"So I would have thought once, and so I am disposed to think now, but I have sometimes thought his bland manners have overcome her Democracy and that somewhere about the premises there is a station; yet 'tis all guess work with me. I give you the information; if you, gentlemen, can make $500 out of it, you are welcome to the fee."

After a short consultation between the constable and the stranger, a regular catcher who had undertaken to capture Jack, they ordered their horses and were off towards the Aughfeultwangher.

VII.

Immediately on receiving Jack into the house, the good landlady supplied him with an ample dish of provisions and removing the dye tub and other obstructions from the pot-hole pointed him to her bedroom for "zingle shentlemens," and when he had disappeared, she replaced her pots and kettles, taking care to place the dye tub in which the yarn for family stockings were receiving its finishing tint of blue, in the very mouth of the hole. This done she went about her morning duties and was thus busily engaged when the two horsemen rode up, dismounted and came in. After paying the compliments of the morning and taking a drink, the constable inquired, "Has Mr. Young been here this morning?"

"Mister Yoong, vat Yoong you means?"

"John Young."

"Vat, dot Shon Yoong fon town in Merzer gounty?"

"Yes."

"O ya, er trive up unt vater ees team."

"Was there anybody with him?"

"O ya, dot black Alec alvays goes mit him."

"Did you see anybody get out?"

"Nein."

"And he didn't leave anyone here?"

"Vell, shentelmens, dot is is von great kweschon. You tinks I have von of tem niggers pout here. You shall zee. Now, shentetmens, you looks all apout; you shall shust go in te barn and dru dis house shust as you blese. Den you knows if Shon Young leaves von black mans here."

So saying the old lady led them through the barn and all parts of the house until the kitchen was reached. Here she bade them look into the oven, and then that they might peer into the pot-hole she began removing the dye tub, but in so doing was careful to spill a little of the liquid. As the fumes spread through the room the catcher exclaimed as they reached his olfactories, " O the d—l.'

"Yes, der toiful, shentelmens, der toiful; you comes to mine house as if de Aughfeultwanger wo'dt keep ein runavay nigger; you go dru, you go unter mine parn; you goes indo mine pet rooms; you climps down into mine shamber, unt you goes up indo mine seller, and now der toiful! You peest tswi tam deeps, unt if you no go so gwick as von leetel minit, I sets mine tok on you unt er makes you into sausage meat fore von hour. Pounce! here Pounce, here!" and a great house dog came rushing into the back door as the two runaway-seekers beat a hasty retreat, each catching a glimpse, as he passed out, of the huge animal called to act as judgment executioner upon them. Though foiled, they were not discouraged, but transferred their place of watching to other parts.

VIII.

Reaching home, Mr. Young immediately wrote Mr. Bishop, as follows:—

"—o— —56—10—28—81.

Dear—— ——,

Piratical craft square rigged, but our wind was good and we *holed* the duck. (— — —) 'Mine Got, mine Got, mine Got——for XXX——' Greeley's advice. Day and night; day and night; day and night. With an eye to foxes, let 'er slide.   Yours,

o ——— o

JACK WATSON. 75

On its receipt, Mr. Bishop took the necessary precautions to execute the contents of the letter, and on the third night proceeded to carry them out, being not unaware of the fact that he was closely watched.

IX.

Two men were standing in their respective doorways in the village of Andover, Ohio, on a November afternoon. The one was a broad-shouldered, full-chested man, with a flowing beard, a merry twinkle in the eye, a kind of devil-me-care negligence in his appearance, with a physique that betokened great power and endurance. This man had long been known technically as "Thribble X" of station "1001," at Gustavus, Ohio, from which place he had migrated to Andover to proclaim the principles of the Universalist faith, and was known among his people as Elder Shipman, or more familiarly, "Uncle Charley."

The other gentleman was of slimmer build, sandy complexion, thoughtful mien, and the very manner in which he handled his pipe would guarantee that he was of "Hinglish stock."

As they thus stood, a buggy came driving from the east at break-neck speed, and dashing up to the parsonage the driver exclaimed, "Elder, can you do anything for this duck, for they're after us hotter'n h—ll."

"Don't you know there is no such place as that, Mose?" was the calm reply.

"Well, well, I've no time to discuss theological matters now; all I know is if there is no such place, there ought to be a new creation at once for the sake of two fellows that must already be this side of the Shenango."

"So near as that? Set him out."

Immediately the colored man was bidden to alight, and whilst he and the elder struck out for the woods a short distance to the southwest, the buggy was turned and driven rapidly toward Richmond.

Scarcely was it out of sight, when two horsemen came galloping into town, and riding up to our English friend, who had been an interested spectator of the little scene just described and was wont to express his satisfaction of English laws by quoting,

"Slaves can not breathe in Highland; if there lungs
Received 'er hair, that moment they are free;"

and inquired, "Stranger, did you see a buggy drive into town from the east a short time ago with two men in it?"

"Hi 'ave, gentlemen."

"Was one of them black?"

"'E was, gentlemen."

"Should you think the other was the man they call Mose Bishop?"

"Hi should, gentlemen."

"Which way did he drive?"

"To the north, gentlemen."

"Thank you, sir, and good day."

"Good day, gentlemen."

Clapping spurs to their horses, the riders were away with a bound, under the inspiration of the first genuine cry of "On to Richmond."

Reaching the proper point, Bishop turned eastward and dashed down through Padan-aram, much to the surprise of the denizens of that sequestered community, whilst his pursuers swept on to the Center, and on inquiry at the village store, were blandly informed by the proprietor, Mr. Heath, that there had been no buggy at all in the place that day. Had Mose and the elder heard the *refined* language that then made the very atmosphere about Richmond blue, they would both have been converts to the orthodox doctrine of sulphuric cleansing.

X.

Watching the departure of the others, Shipman and his charge crossed the road to the eastward, and were soon threading the woodlands bordering the Shenango, and about midnight sought quarters at a friend's of the elder, not far from Linesville. Arming themselves with heavy walking sticks, just before evening of the next day they set out for Albion. They had not proceeded far before they saw they were to encounter four sinister-looking fellows. "Now, Jack," said the elder, "You have endured too much to be taken back. I do not wish to pay a thousand dollars fine nor go to prison for your sake. We may have to use these canes. Do you understand?"

"Yes, Massa, you can trus' dis Jack."

A call to halt was answered by so vigorous a charge and such effective use of the walking sticks that two of the challengers soon lay upon the ground and the others beat a hasty retreat. Taking advantage of circumstances the little train switched, and under the pressure of a full head of steam reached the "Old Tannery" station near Albion before daylight.

The conductor was now on strange ground, but knowing there was an agent in the vicinity named Low, he hunted him up and received such information as enabled them to make a little clump of hemlocks on the bank of a ravine not far from the residence of Elijah Drury, of Girard, the following night.

Farmer Drury was a stalwart, standing little less than six feet in height, always ready for any good word and work, and had been for many years engaged in the *transportation* business. Always wary, however, he was not to be deceived when, in the morning, our bewhiskered conductor presented himself and asked for something to eat.

"O yes," said Mr. Drury, "I can always furnish a man, though a stranger, something with which to satisfy hunger."

"But I want something also for a friend."

"A friend! What do you mean?"

"I mean that I have a friend down yonder in the thicket, who is both weary and hungry."

JACK WATSON.

"Mister, do you know what I think?"

"I am not a prophet, sir."

"Well, it is my opinion that you are a horse thief."

"Will you come down and see the last nag I trotted off?"

Together the two men went down to the little thicket, and there the Elder not only exhibited the passenger, but to remove all suspicions, showed him the scars that indicated the floggings to which the slave had been subjected, a sight which Mr. Drury often afterwards said came very near making him swear outright. Thus commenced a friendship between the two men long continued and fraught with many acts attesting the generous nature of both.

XI.

When evening came, time being precious, our conductor drew the reins over Mr. Drury's best roadsters, and about midnight deposited his passenger at the doorway of an old-fashioned house, with gable to the street, wing projecting northward, and a large elm tree nearly in front, standing on Federal Hill, in what is now South Erie, and for the first time XXX greeted officially a most redoubtable Keystone agent, known as the "Doctor," in those days one of Erie's well-known characters. He had gained some knowledge of herbs and roots, which he learned to apply medicinally, thus acquiring his appellation, which he wore with great satisfaction, soon coming to look upon all mere "book doctors" in great contempt. He was accustomed to drive about town with an old brown horse attached to a kind of carry-all vehicle; always took his whisky straight and in full allopathic doses, though he affected to despise the practice generally, and prided himself on being the most *reliable agent* in Erie county.

Into the Doctor's private sanctum Jack was at once admitted, and properly cared for for a number of days, until measurably recuperated from his weeks of incessant vigil and solicitude, when he was taken in charge by Thomas Elliott, Esq., of Harborcreek, and conveyed to Wesleyville, four miles east of the city. Here, inasmuch as fresh news was obtained of his pursuers, it was thought best to secrete him anew, and he was therefore deposited in Station "Sanctum Sanctorum"—the garret of the Methodist Church.

Whoever passes through the village on the "Buffalo Road," fails not to notice this unpretentious little brick structure standing by the wayside. Like most churches built so long ago, it has undergone various remodelings. The "battlements" have been taken off; doors and windows have shifted places, but within it is little changed; the seating below and the three-sided gallery remaining much as of old.

From the time of its first dedication onward, it has been the scene of many a revival, and for years it was the "horn of the altar" upon which the panting fugitive laid his hand, and was safe, for its use as a "station" was known only to a "selected few."

OLD CHURCH, WESLEYVILLE, PA.

JACK WATSON.   81

At the time we speak of, a protracted meeting had already been begun, for the bleakness of winter had early set in. The services were conducted by Rev. Jas. Gilfillin, a sterling old Scotchman, who had received a large part of his training in the collieries of his native land, and before the mast as a sailor on the high seas, assisted by Rev. William Gheer, a young man of timidity and all gentility of manner. The interest was most marked, and crowds came nightly to listen, to weep, to become penitents, not only from up and down the "road," but from Gospel Hill, and far beyond, bringing even grand old father and mother Weed, who had assisted at the formation of the society over thirty years before, from away up in the "beechwoods," and with them Nehemiah Beers, an exhorter, particularly felicitious in the construction of unheard-of words and expressions.

Under such circumstances Jack was deposited, early one morning, in his rude apartment, measurably warmed by the pipe which came up from the great box-stove below, and cautioned that he must keep particularly quiet during the devotional exercises below. Here he remained for several days, listening to the praises of new-born souls and the hosannas of the older brethren during meeting hours, and then descending and making himself comfortable in the well-warmed room when all was quiet and safe. Indeed, so well did he play his part as fire-tender, that the Chambers boys, who chopped the wood, which was hauled to the church "sled-length" by the brethren, emphatically declared, as they wondered at the marvellous disappearance of fuel, "It takes a power of wood to run a red-hot revival, and we shall be glad when the meeting closes," and it required no little effort on the part of their father, the main source of supply, to induce them to persevere in their "labor of love."

Thus matters passed until Sunday evening came, when the interest of the meeting seemed to culminate in a Pentecostal shower. The Rev. James Sullivan, then a young man, preached a sermon of great eloquence and power, encouraged by many a hearty Amen from Father Weed and the older brethren, and the responsive hallelujahs of hale old Sister Weed and the other "Mothers in Israel." The sermon ended, men clapped their hands in ecstatic rapture, and struck up that grand old revival hymn,

"Come ye sinners, poor and needy,"

whilst the old pastor rose in his place, and earnestly exhorted sinners to come to the "mourner's bench" and find pardon and peace, until the feeling of excitement burst forth in one simultaneous, "Amen, hallelujah to God!"

The Spirit had reached the garret, and in the fervor of excitement Jack forgot himself, and, "Amen, hallelujah to God!" came back in responsive echo, sufficiently loud enough to attract the attention of those in the gallery, who looked at each other in startled amazement.

Down on his knees went Brother Beers, and in the midst of an impassioned prayer, exclaimed: "O! Lord-ah, come down to night-ah, and rim-wrack and center-shake the work of the devil-ah."

Influenced more by the Spirit than the phraseology of the prayer, there went up from the worshipping throng a hearty "Amen, and Amen!"

"Amen, and Amen!" came down from above, only to increase the astonishment of the crowded gallery, most there believing that an angel hovered over them. As if in perfect accord with the surroundings, Parson Gheer struck up,

"Behold the Savior of mankind,"

without waiting for

"Nailed to the rugged cross,"

the sentorian voice of the old pastor rang out, "Yes, He comes! He comes!"

"Yes, He comes! He comes!" shouted the embodied seraph in the garret, in tones sufficiently loud to catch the ear of the sexton, who immediately mounted aloft, as he often did to adjust the stovepipe, and though the meeting continued for an hour longer, there were no farther angelic demonstrations, yet some in the gallery long persisted that they had that night been permitted to listen to seraphic strains.

Before daylight Jack was shipped by way of Col. Moorhead's and North East, to Conductor Nutting, at State Line, and by him to Syracuse, where he safely arrived and remained until the breaking out of the war, when he went south and rendered valuable service to the Union cause, in a way that may be told in due time.

CHAPTER III.

UNCLE JAKE.

I.

YEARS ago, before the permanent organization of the Underground Railroad, when the escape of fugitives was largely a haphazard matter, there lived on the sacred soil of Virginia, back a few miles from Wheeling, a pleasant, companionable man, owning a number of slaves, among them one known as "Uncle Jake," the happy husband of an exemplary wife, who had borne him several children, some of whom they had seen grow to manhood and womanhood, while others still remained with them in the cabin.

Uncle Jake was an expert mason, and brought his master large wages. The latter, in the generosity of his heart, had stipulated that a certain per cent. of these should be credited up to Jake for the purchase of the freedom of himself and wife. When he turned his fifty-ninth birthday the sum agreed upon was nearly reached, and the faithful man went out to a job in Wheeling, with the full assurance that on his sixtieth anniversary he and his hale old wife should go forth to the enjoyment of the blessings of free people. Thus incited, his trowel was nimbly handled as the days flew by.

A little improvident and immethodical in his business, the master had contracted large obligations, which he was unable to meet; his paper matured; his creditors swooped down upon him simultaneously, and in a single day he was stripped of everything. His slaves, with the exception of Uncle Jake, who was purchased at a round figure by a neighbor who had long coveted him, were sold to a southern trader, and on Saturday morning, chained into separate coffles, the unhappy wife and mother, with her children, forming one by themselves, whilst the father, indulging in pleasant day-dreams of the future, was busily plying his craft in one part of the town, were driven through another, down to the river, and put on board a steamer for New Orleans.

Evening came, and the week's work ended, Uncle Jake started with a light heart homeward. When he reached the neighborhood sometime after nightfall, he was apprised by a friend on the look-out for him, of the fate of the master—of himself and loved ones. Had a thunderbolt fallen at his feet, he could not have been more shocked. Learning, also, that his new master, a tyrannical man, was waiting his coming, he turned aside to give vent to his grief. Had he been sold with the family he could have endured it, for then there might have been a chance of occasional meeting; indeed, he and his wife might have been sold to the same plantation; but now they were gone—separated forever. Under the blue dome of heaven, with the myriad stars looking down upon him, he wept—wept as only a man can weep under such circumstances—until the reaction came, when a lion-like manhood asserted itself in the laconic expression, "Not one more stroke in slavery."

Arising with the clear-cut resolution to obtain his freedom or perish in the attempt, he proceeded stealthily to his cabin, armed himself with a large butcher knife and a heavy walking stick, and taking one last look at objects, though humble, still dear to him, he set out with elastic step towards the river. About one-half the distance had been gone over, when he perceived himself pursued. He turned aside, hoping to secrete himself, but in vain; he had been sighted, and was summoned to surrender.

To the challenge, he responded: "I am yours if you can take me."

The two men, his new master and an attendant, dismounted and hitched their horses, thinking the conquest of the "cowardly nigger" would be an easy matter. But not so. The man who for nearly three-score years had manifested only the meakness of a child, was now endowed with the spirit and prowess of a giant. A well-aimed blow of the bludgeon laid his master a quivering corpse at his feet, and several well-directed strokes of the butcher knife sent the other covered with ghastly, bleeding wounds, fainting to the roadside.

Mounting the fleetest horse, Jake made his way

rapidly to the river, and plunging in soon found himself landed safely on the Ohio shore. Taking to a highway soon found, he followed the lead of the north star, and just at daybreak turned into a woodland ravine, and spent the quiet autumnal Sabbath watching the grazing of the faithful horse upon such herbage as he could find, and in meditating upon the wonderful revelations and events of the past twenty-four hours.

Night clear and beautiful, came again, and Jake pursued his onward way, and in the early morning turned his jaded beast loose in a retired pasture lot not far from Salem; threw the saddle and bridle into a ravine, on the principle that "dead men tell no tales," and prospecting about for some time, saw emerge from a farm house a broad-brimmed hat, which he had learned was a sure sign of food and protection. Approaching the Quaker farmer, Uncle Jake declared himself a fugitive, and applied for food and shelter, which were freely granted.

Tuesday the stage coach brought into Salem a handbill giving a full description of Uncle Jake, telling of the killing of the master, the probable mortal wounding of the other, and offering a large reward for his apprehension.

"Thee oughtest to have struck more carefully, friend," said the Quaker, when he had learned thus fully the measure of his protégé's adventure, "but then as it was in the dark, we may pardon thee thy error, but Salem is not a safe place for such as thee.

UNCLE JAKE. 89

I shall take thee to my friend, Dr. Benjamin Stanton, who will instruct thee as to what thee is to do."

Accordingly, when nightfall made it safe, the Quaker took Jake to the house of his friend, who was none other than a cousin of Lincoln's great War Secretary, where having exchanged his laborer's garb for a suit of army blue, richly trimmed with brass buttons, a style of dress much admired by colored people in those old days of militia training, and a high-crowned hat, he was immediately posted off to the care of one Barnes, residing on the confines of Boardman, bearing to him the simple admonition, " It is hot."

Not appreciating the full merits of the case, Barnes took him in the early morning and started for Warren by way of Youngstown. Here he was espied by two questionable characters, who having seen the hand-bill advertising Jake, and knowing the antecedents of Barnes, justly surmised that the black gentleman in blue might be none other than the individual for whom the reward was offered, and at once planned a pursuit, but not until the eagle eye of the driver had detected their motions. Leaving the main road, he struck across the Liberty hills. When near Loy's Corners he perceived they were pursued, and bade Jake alight and make for some place of safety, while he would try and lead the pursuers off the trail.

In a land of strangers and without protective weapons save his knife, Jake could do nothing more than to run up to a little wagon shop by the wayside, in the doorway of which stood an honest Pennsylvania Dutchman named Samuel Goist, and exclaimed, "Lor' Massa, save me from the slave catcher."

Now, Mr. Goist was a Democrat of the straightest sect, and had long sworn by "Sheneral Shackson;" he had never before seen a panting fugitive and knew nothing of secretive methods, but when he saw the venerable, though unique form before him, his generous heart was touched, and he replied: "Hite gwick in ter hay yonder till I cums," pointing at the same time to a last year's haystack, into which the cattle had eaten deep recesses.

It was but the work of a moment, and sable form, blue suit and plug hat were viewless in what the winter before had often sheltered the semi-farmer's choicest steer from pitiless storm.

Scarcely was this feat executed when the Youngstown parties came up and knowing the political complexion of the honest wagon-maker inquired, "Halloo, old dad, have you seen a buggy go by here with a white man, and a nigger dressed in blue, in it?"

"Ya, shentlemen, py shimmeny; dot puggy vent py das corner ond yonder not more as den minit aco, unt er vas *trifing* das horse, py shingo. I dinks you not oferdakes him much pefore Vorren."

With an expression of rough thanks, the men struck off under a full gallop which carried them into Warren right speedily, but in the meantime

UNCLE JAKE.

Barnes had watched his opportunity, turned off through Niles, and pursued his homeward journey by way of Austintown.

Turning from his shop when his interrogators were out of sight, Mr. Goist called his good frou and said, "Vell, Mutter, I kes I haf lite shust a lidel."

"Vot, you, fater, haf lite? O mine!"

"Vell, Mutter, you zee von plack man comes along unt asks me him for to hite, unt I say in dem stock; unt den cums sum mans fon Youngstown unt says he 'Olt dat, you sees von puggy mit nigger unt vite man goes dis vay?' Unt I say, 'Ya, dot puggy vas kon py like a shtreak.'"

"O mine, fater, das vas no liegen; you shust say dot puggy vas kon."

"Vell, if dot mans was Sheneral Shackson, I should him tell shust der zame."

That evening Uncle Jake received an ample supper from the larder of good Mother Goist, and was then placed in a wagon under a cover of straw and conveyed close to the house of a Mr. Stewart near the corner of Vienna, whom rumor had pointed out to the honest Dutchman as one of "dem aperlishioners." Here he was bidden "goot py," and soon found his way to the cabin indicated, whence in due time he was forwarded to General Andrew Bushnell, a prominent anti-slavery man south of the centre of Hartford.

II.

Even at that early day, Hartford and Vernon had

established for themselves a wide-spread reputation for expertness in the *forwarding business.* General Bushnell, on account of his age and experience was looked upon as the acknowledged front of affairs, but his work was ably seconded by many others, particularly by two young men, Ralph Plumb, of Burgh Hill, and Levi Sutliff, who still resided with his parents in the north part of Vernon. These young men were ever on the alert for daring enterprise, but just now discretion was considered the better part of valor, for slow as news moved, it was not long before the chase from Youngstown to Warren became known in Hartford, and anti-fugitive eyes became unusually vigilant about town, and it was whispered that the blue suit might come that way and some one might pick up a handsome reward.

For some days Uncle Jake was carefully secreted in a hay barn, together with a young man who had previously reached the General's. Plumb and Sutliff were so carefully watched, it was thought best to commit the carrying of the twain to other hands— but whose should they be?

Young Plumb had a sister Mary, about twenty years of age, the affianced of Sutliff, and the General had a daughter bearing the same name a year or two younger, both spirited, resolute girls, and ready for any good work. When only fourteen, Miss Bushnell, in a case of special emergency, had hitched up the family carriage, (a one-horse wagon,) and conveyed a fleeing family from her father's to the Sutliff

UNCLE JAKE. 93

home, a distance of eight miles, encountering a fearful thunderstorm on the way, and returning before the first peep of morning light.

One day when conversing on the best way of disposing of the case in hand, Ralph said: "Leve, suppose we commit this mission to the Marys; I believe they will put the stock safely through to the lake."

"Capital," replied his companion; "have you matured a scheme?"

"Partially."

"What is it?"

"Well your father is to have a load of hay of the General. Come along with the team and I'll help you get it. We'll pack Uncle Jake and the boy into the load, take Mary on with us and bring her down to our house, there take on sister, and when the hay is in the Sutliff barn the rest can be easily arranged."

"But will the girls consent?"

"The Bushnell has been tried, and you are the last man that ought to raise a question about the Plumb."

That afternoon the team of the senior Sutliff was driven through the center of Hartford and to the hay-barn of Andrew Bushnell, where it was duly loaded, the two choicest *spires* being extended longitudinally a short distance from the top. Passing the house, Mary was taken on and a merry trio proceeded northward only to be expanded to a jubilant quartette on arriving at the Hill. No suspicion was aroused, for those were days when a woman's worth and modesty were not lessened by her being seen in sun-bonnet and shawl upon a load of hay.

III.

One, two, three, ——, ——, ——, ——, ——, ——, ——, ——, twelve, went the clock in the old, low Sutliff mansion; a light two-horse wagon, the bed filled with hay as if covering a "grist," was backed out of the barn; two strong horses were attached; warm kisses were administered to ruby lips; and a couple of well-wrapped female forms ascended to the seat; a delicately gloved hand laid hold of the lines, and the team sped briskly towards the "Kinsman woods."

IV.

Deacon Andrews, in the old farm house still standing on the brink of the little ravine south of the hamlet of Lindenville, had put up his morning prayer for the drowning host of Pharaoh, the Greeks, the Romans and the Jews, said "Amen" and arisen from his knees, when his wife, looking out of the window, exclaimed: "See, husband, there's the Sutliff team; but who is driving? As I live, if it isn't a couple of girls, and all the way up from Vernon so early as this! What can they want?"

"Going to the 'Harbor' with *grain*, I presume; likely the men folks are busy."

"But then I didn't know the Sutliff's have any girls."

"Well, wife, likely they've hired the team to some of the neighbors. You start the children out after chestnuts, quick."

There was a lively scampering of young Andrews to the woods; a hasty breakfasting of girls and horses; a close examination of the sacks under the hay to see if all was right; a pleasant "good morning," and the team went northward and the deacon to his work, mentally exclaiming: "Great and marvelous are the works of the Almighty—and Plumb and Sut—" but he checked the irreverent conclusion.

V.

It was high noon at Jefferson, and Ben Wade brought his fist down upon the cover of the volume of Blackstone he had closed, as he arose to go to dinner, and ejaculated, "Who the d—l is that, Gid."

The pleasant, bland countenanced gentleman to whom these words were addresssd looked up, and there in front of the little office bearing the unpretentious sign,

"GIDDINGS & WADE,
ATTORNEYS AT LAW."

were two plump, rosy-cheeked girls, each engaged in hitching a horse.

"Zounds, Ben, you ought to know your Trumbull county friends. It hasn't been so long since you taught school at the Center of Hartford that you should have forgotten the Bushnells and the Plumbs."

"The h—ll! I wonder if those two lasses can be the little Mollies I used to enjoy so much."

"They are the Miss Bushnell and Miss Plumb I met at Sutliff's a few days ago, though I do not know their names."

The two attorneys, as yet unknown to fame, attended, without fees, to the consultation of the young ladies, treated them and theirs to the best fare of him who was afterwards well known in *Railroad* circles as "Anno Mundi," and then sent them forward with a kind letter of introduction to "Doctor" Henry Harris, the most likely man to greet them.

VI.

"Can you direct us to Dr. Harris?" said a sweet voiced girl to a trim, quick-stepping, rather fashionably dressed young gentleman on the street in the little village of Ashtabula, as she reined up a two-horse team.

"Hem, 'em 'em, Dr. Harris? 'em, why, that is what they call me."

"Are you the only Dr. Harris in town?"

"'Em, yes, Miss. What can I do for you?"

The letters of the Jefferson attorneys was placed in his hands.

"'Em, hem," he exclaimed, after reading it. "*Freight!* we can not ship now; shall have to stow it in our up-town ware-house;" saying which he led the way out to a country home, now occupied as a city residence, where the freight was deposited in a hay mow, whilst the kind-hearted old Scotchman, Deacon McDonald and his wife most graciously cared for the intrepid drivers for the night.

UNCLE JAKE. 97

The young man Ned was soon sent away, but Uncle Jake lingered in the vicinity for considerable time. The winter of 1836 he spent at the Harbor in the family of Deacon Wm. Hubbard, rendering valuable service in "pointing" the walls and plastering the cellar of the house now occupied as a store and residence by Captain Starkey. He is still well remembered by A. F. Hubbard, Esq., whose father offered him a home in his family; but Jake finally left and nothing is known of his subsequent course.

Of the two young ladies so intimately connected with this history, Miss Bushnell ultimately married a Mr. Estabrook, and was for many years one of the most esteemed ladies of Warren, O., and now sleeps in Oakwood Cemetery near that beautiful city. The other joined her destiny with that of her affiance shortly after that memorable ride, and a few weeks since I stood in the little church-yard at Burgh Hill, shrouded as it was in a far-reaching coverlet of snow and copied the following from a small marble headstone:

"MARY P. SUTLIFF,
Died March 1st, 1836.
AE., 23.
First Sec'y of the Female Anti-Slavery Society of Vernon, A. D., 1834."

CHAPTER IV.

GEORGE GREEN,

OR CONSTANCY REWARDED.

[The circumstances of the following narative were partially written up when secured by the author.]

"DO you believe you can succeed, George? It is a great undertaking."

"If we can not succeed, Mary, we can try. This servitude is worse than death."

"But our master is very good."

"Yes, master is good and kind, and no harm shall come to him. But no master is as good as freedom."

"But then the whites have all the power on their side."

"The whites, Mary! Who are whiter than we—than you and I? You the slave of your own father; I sold from my mother's arms that my features might not bring disgrace upon a man of position. White folks, indeed!"

"True, George, our lot is a wretched one, but then as you love me, and as master and mistress are so kind, would it not be better to remain quiet, lest we, too, are separated, and all our hopes for life blighted?"

"We are taking a great risk, Mary, but Nat says

GEORGE GREEN.

we can not fail. I sometimes fear that we shall and I know the consequences, and will meet them like a man, for I know you will love me still, Mary."

"Yes, George, but the love of a poor helpless slave girl can not compensate you for what you may have to endure, perhaps for life itself."

"Mary, dear as you are to me, liberty for us both, or death in attempting to secure it, will be a far greater boon, coupled with your love, than to share that love, however fervent, through a life-long servitude."

"But, George, don't you remember how often you have heard master and his guests talk about those strange people, Poles and Greeks they call them, and how they have struggled for freedom, only mostly to make their condition worse?"

"Yes, Mary, and I have heard them tell how they would like to go and help them fight for their liberty. Then I have heard master tell how his own father fought in the war he calls the Revolution, and didn't the Judge say in his speech last Independence that that is the day, above all others, which proclaims that 'all men are created free and equal?' Am I not a man, and should I not be equal to any one who calls himself master and me slave? No, Mary, the die is cast and six hundred slaves—no, men—will strike for freedom on these plantations in less than a week. But there is the horn, and I must go."

The above conversation took place in the home of a Virginia planter more than sixty years ago. The parties were young, less than twenty; both white, both slaves, for the peculiar institution by no means attached itself to the sable African alone. The fettered were of every hue, from that of ebon blackness to the purest caucassion white. Slavery knew no sacred ties, but only the bonds of lust. Hence this strange gradation of color, for as the master acknowledged nothing more than a conventional marriage, so he held out no encouragement to the slave women to be virtuous and chaste. The girl Mary was, indeed, the daughter of Mr. Green, her master, and George the son of a high government official, his mother being a servant in the Washington hotel where the official boarded. The boy looked so akin to his father that he was early sold to a slave dealer that the scandal might be hushed. From this dealer he was purchased by Mr. Green, who was indeed a kind-hearted man and treated his slaves with great consideration.

Both being house servants, and thrown much together, an earnest attachment sprang up between them. This was by no means discouraged by master or mistress. Though they could neither read nor write, their natural aptness and constant association with family and guests soon imparted to them a good degree of culture and general information.

The cause of the conversation above referred to was the revelation to Mary by her lover of a plot on the part of about six hundred slaves of the county of Southampton to rise in rebellion and obtain their

GEORGE GREEN.

freedom. From any participation in it she would gladly have dissuaded him, though in perfect sympathy with his feelings, but the proud Anglo-Saxon blood and spirit of George were fully enlisted in the undertaking, and when "Nat Turner's Insurrection" broke upon the astonished planters there was no braver man in its ranks than George. But six hundred slaves, imperfectly armed as they were, could make but little headway. They were soon defeated. Those who were not captured fled to the Dismal Swamp. Here ordered to surrender, they challenged their pursuers. A furious struggle ensued between the owners and their human chattels, men and women. They were hunted with blood-hounds, and many who were caught were tortured even unto death. Not until the United States troops were called in, was their forlorn hope, struggling for freedom, entirely vanquished.

Among the last to surrender was George. He was tried before a civil court and condemned to be hanged. Ten days only were to elapse before the carrying out of the sentence.

Being a member of a Christian church, Mary sought and obtained, through the influence of her mistress, with whom George had been an especial favorite, permission to visit him in the jail and administer the consolation of religion. Seated by his side but four days before the day of execution, she said:

"George you made an effort for freedom against

my wish, now will you make another, one in which I fully accord?"

"For me there is no hope. Whilst it is hard to part from you, I am not afraid to die."

"If you are hanged, we must be separated, if you escape it can be no more."

"Escape! how?"

"Well, listen. You shall exchange clothes with me. Then at my accustomed time of leaving you shall depart, and I will remain in your place. They will not harm me, and so nearly are we of a size, and so close the general resemblance, that you will have no difficulty in passing the guard. Once without the gate, you can easily escape to the woods, the mountains, to a land of liberty. May be——"

"Never can I consent to this. These miserable men would wreak their vengeance on you."

"Never fear for me, and may be when you are safe in Canada you can provide for my coming to you."

"If it were possible, but—"

The turnkey gave the signal for departure, and Mary arose and left.

During the next day she carefully prepared a package of provisions and hid it in a secluded place. The day was dark and gloomy, portending a storm. Just at evening she presented herself at the prison door and was readily admitted. Once beside her lover, she again importuned him to make an effort to escape. At last he consented. It was but the work of a moment to exchange clothing, to impart the necessary instructions with regard to the provisions, to pledge one another to eternal constancy, when the door opened and the harsh voice of the keeper exclaimed, "Come, Miss, it is time for you to go."

It was now storming furiously. Weeping and with a handkerchief applied to his face, as was Mary's custom when leaving, George passed out and the door immediately closed upon the innocent inmate of the cell.

It was now dark, so that our hero in his new dress had no fear of detection. The provisions were sought and found, and poor George was soon on the road to Canada. But neither he nor Mary had thought of a change of dress for him when he should have escaped, and he walked but a short distance before he felt that a change of his apparel would facilitate his progress. But he dared not go among even his colored associates, for fear of being betrayed. However, he made the best of his way on towards Canada, hiding in the woods by day and traveling by the guidance of the pole star at night.

One morning George arrived on the banks of the Ohio river, and found his journey had terminated unless he could get some one to take him across in a secret manner, for he would not be permitted to cross in any of the ferry boats. He concealed himself in tall grass and weeds near the river to see if he could not secure an opportunity to cross. He had been in his hiding place but a short time, when he observed a man in a small boat, floating near the shore, evidently fishing. His first impulse was to call out to the man and ask him to take him across the river to the Ohio shore, but the fear that he was a slaveholder or one who might possibly arrest him deterred him from it. The man after rowing and floating about for some time, fastened the boat to the root of a tree, and started to a farm-house not far distant. This was George's opportunity, and he seized it. Running down the bank, he unfastened the boat and jumped in, and with all the expertness of one accustomed to a boat, rowed across the river and landed safely on free soil.

Being now in a free state, he thought he might with perfect safety travel on towards Canada. He had, however, gone but a few miles, when he discovered two men on horseback coming behind him. He felt sure that they could not be in pursuit of him, yet he did not wish to be seen by them, so he turned into another road leading to a house near by. The men followed, and were but a short distance from George, when he ran up to a farm-house, before which was standing a farmer-looking man, in a broad-brimmed hat and straight-collared coat, whom he implored to save him from the "slave-catchers." The farmer told him to go into the barn near by; he entered by the front door, the farmer following and closing the door behind George, but remaining outside, gave directions to his hired man as to what

GEORGE GREEN.

should be done with him. The slaveholders had by this time dismounted, and were in front of the barn demanding admittance, and charging the farmer with secreting their slave woman, for George was still in the dress of a woman. The Friend, for the farmer proved to be a member of the Society of Quakers, told the slave-owners that if they wished to search his barn, they must first get an officer and a search warrant. While the parties were disputing, the farmer began nailing up the front door, and the hired man served the back door the same way. The slaveholders, finding that they could not prevail on the Friend to allow them to get the slave, determined to go in search of an officer. One was left to see that the slave did not escape from the barn, while the other went off at full speed to Mt. Pleasant, the nearest town.

George was not the slave of either of these men, nor were they in pursuit of him, but they had lost a woman who had been seen in that vicinity, and when they saw poor George in the disguise of a female, and attempting to elude pursuit, they felt sure they were close upon their victim. However, if they had caught him, although he was not their slave they would have taken him back and placed him in jail, and there he would have remained until his owner arrived.

After an absence of nearly two hours, the slave-owner returned with an officer, and found the Friend still driving large nails into the door. In a triumphant tone, and with a corresponding gesture, he handed the search-warrant to the Friend, and said:

"There, sir, now I will see if he can't get my Nigger."

"Well," said the Friend, "thou hast gone to work according to law, and thou canst now go into my barn."

"Lend me your hammer that I may get the door open," said the slaveholder."

"Let me see the warrant again." And after reading it over once more, he said, "I see nothing in this paper which says I must supply thee with tools to open my door; if thou wishest to go in thou must get a hammer elsewhere."

The sheriff said: "I will go to a neighboring farm and borrow something which will introduce us to Miss Dinah;" and he immediately went off in search of tools.

In a short time the officer returned, and they commenced an assault and battery upon the barn door, which soon yielded; and in went the slaveholder and officer, and began turning up the hay and using all other means to find the lost property; but, to their astonishment, the slave was not there. After all hopes of getting Dinah were gone, the slave-owner, in a rage, said to the Friend:

"My Nigger is not here."

"I did not tell thee there was anyone here."

"Yes, but I saw her go in, and you shut the door behind her, and if she wa'nt in the barn what did you nail the door for?"

"Can not I do what I please with my own barn door? Now I will tell thee. Thou need trouble thyself no more, for the person thou art after entered the front door and went out the back door, and is a long way from here by this time Thou and thy friend must be somewhat fatigued by this time; won't thee go in and take a little dinner with me?"

We need not say that this cool invitation of the good Quaker was not accepted by the slaveholders.

George in the meantime had been taken to a Friend's dwelling some miles away, where, after laying aside his female attire, and being snugly dressed up in a straight-collared coat, and pantaloons to match, he was again put on the right road towards Canada.

His passage through Ohio, by the way of Canfield and Warren, was uneventful, but at Bloomfield he was detained several days on account of the presence of some slave hunters from his own state, and who had a description of him among others. In this town is a great marsh or swamp of several thousand acres, at the time of our story all undrained. In the center of this swamp, Mr. Brown, the owner, had erected a small hut, one of the very first special stations built on the Underground Railroad. To this secluded retreat George was taken, and there remained until the departure of his enemies, when he was safely conveyed to Ashtabula Harbor, whence he was given free passage, by the veteran agent, Hubbard, of the Mystic Line in Canada. Arriving at St. Catherines, he began to work upon the farm of Colonel Strut, and also attended a night school, where he showed great proficiency in acquiring the rudiments of an education.

Once beginning to earn money, George did not forget his promise to use all means in his power to get Mary out of slavery. He, therefore, labored with all his might to obtain money with which to employ some one to go back to Virginia for Mary. After nearly six month's labor at St. Catharines, he employed an English missionary to go and see if the girl could be purchased, and at what price. The missionary went accordingly, but returned with the sad intelligence that on account of Mary's aiding George to escape, the court had compelled Mr. Green to sell her out of the State, and she had been sold to a Negro-trader and taken to the New Orleans market. As all hope of getting the girl was now gone, George resolved to quit the American continent forever. He immediately took passage in a vessel laden with timber, bound for Liverpool, and in five weeks from the time he was standing on a quay of the great English seaport. With little education, he found many difficulties in the way of getting a respectable living. However, he obtained a situation as porter in a large house in Manchester, where he worked during the day, and took private lessons at night. In this way he labored for three years, and was then raised to the position of clerk. George was so white as easily to pass for Caucassian, and being

GEORGE GREEN.

somewhat ashamed of his African decent, he never once mentioned the fact of his having been a slave. He soon became a partner in the firm that employed him, and was now on the road to wealth.

In the year 1842, just ten years after, George Green, for so he called himself, arrived in England, he visited France, and spent some days at Dunkirk.

It was towards sunset, on a warm day in the month of October, that Mr. Green, after strolling some distance from the Hotel de Leon, entered a burial ground and wandered long alone among the silent dead, gazing upon the many green graves and marble tombstones of those who once moved on the theatre of busy life, and whose sounds of gayety once fell upon the ear of man. All nature was hushed in silence, and seemed to partake of the general melancholy which hung over the quiet resting-place of departed mortals. After tracing the varied inscriptions which told the characters or conditions of the departed, and viewing the mounds beneath which the dust of mortality slumbered, he had reached a secluded spot, near to where an aged weeping willow bowed its thick foliage to the ground, as though anxious to hide from the scrutinizing gaze of curiosity the grave beneath it. Mr. Green seated himself upon a marble tomb, and began to read Roscoe's Leo X., a copy of which he had under his arm. It was then about twilight, and he had scarcely read half a page, when he observed a lady dressed in black, and leading a boy some five years old up one of the paths; and as the lady's black veil was over her face, he felt somewhat at liberty to eye her more closely. While looking at her, the lady gave a scream and appeared to be in a fainting position, when Mr. Green sprang from his seat in time to save her from falling to the ground. At this moment an elderly gentleman was seen approaching with a rapid step, who, from his appearance, was evidently the lady's father, or one intimately connected with her. He came up, and in a confused manner asked what was the matter. Mr. Green explained as well as he could. After taking up the smelling bottle, which had fallen from her hand, and holding it a short time to her face, she soon began to revive. During all this time the lady's veil had so covered her face that Mr. Green had not seen it. When she had so far recovered as to be able to raise her head, she again screamed, and fell back in the arms of the old man. It now appeared quite certain that either the countenance of George Green, or some other object, was the cause of these fits of fainting; and the old gentleman, thinking it was the former, in rather a petulant tone, said, "I will thank you, sir, if you will leave us alone." The child whom the lady was leading had now set up a squall; and amid the death-like appearance of the lady, the harsh look of the old man, and the cries of the boy, Mr. Green left the grounds and returned to his hotel.

Whilst seated by the window, and looking out upon the crowded street, with every now and then the strange scene in the graveyard vividly before him, Mr. Green thought of the book he had been reading, and remembering that he had left it on the tomb, where he had suddenly dropped it when called to the assistance of the lady, he immediately determined to return in search of it. After a walk of some twenty minutes, he was again over the spot where he had been an hour before, and from where he had been so uncermoniously expelled by the old man. He looked in vain for the book; it was nowhere to be found; nothing save the bouquet which the lady had dropped, and which lay half buried in the grass from having been trodden upon, indicated that any one had been there that evening. Mr. Green took up the bunch of flowers, and again returned to the hotel.

After passing a sleepless night, and hearing the clock strike six, he dropped into a sweet sleep, from which he did not awake until roused by the rap of a servant, who, entering the room, handed him a note which ran as follows:—

"Sir: I owe an apology for the inconvenience to which you were subjected last evening, and if you will honor us with your presence to dinner to-day at four o'clock, I shall be most happy to give you due satisfaction. My servant will be in waiting for you at half-past three.

I am, sir, your obedient servant,

J. DEVENANT.

To George Green, Esq.　　　　　　October 23."

The servant who handed this note to Mr. Green informed him that the bearer was waiting for a reply. He immediately resolved to accept the invitation, and replied accordingly. Who this person was, and how his name and hotel where he was stopping had been found out, was indeed a mystery. However, he waited somewhat impatiently for the hour when he was to see his new acquaintance, and get the mysterious meeting in the grave-yard solved.

The clock on the neighboring church had scarcely ceased striking three, when the servant announced that a carriage had called for Mr. Green. In less than half an hour he was seated in a most sumptuous barouche, drawn by two beautiful iron grays, and rolling along over a splendid gravel road, completely shaded by large trees which appeared to have been the accumulated growth of centuries. The carriage soon stopped in front of a low villa, and this too was imbedded in magnificent trees covered with moss. Mr. Green alighted and was shown into a superb drawing-room, the walls of which were hung with fine specimens from the hands of the great Italian painters, and one by a German artist representing a beautiful monkish legend connected with "The Holy Catharine," an illustrious lady of Alexandra. The furniture had an antique and dignified appearance. High-backed chairs stood around the room; a venerable mirror stood on the mantle shelf; rich curtains of crimson damask hung in folds at either side of the large windows; and a rich Turkish carpet covered the floor. In the center stood a table covered with books, in the midst of which was an old-fashioned vase filled with fresh flowers, whose fragrance was exceedingly pleasant. A faint light, together with the quietness of the hour, gave a beauty, beyond description, to the whole scene.

Mr. Green had scarcely seated himself upon the sofa, when the elderly gentleman whom he had met the previous evening made his appearance, followed by the little boy, and introduced himself as Mr. Devenant. A moment more, and a lady—a beautiful brunette—dressed in black, with long curls of a chestnut color hanging down her cheeks, entered the room. Her eyes were of a dark hazel, and her whole appearance indicated that she was a native of a southern clime. The door at which she entered was opposite to where the two gentlemen were seated. They immediately arose; and Mr. Devenant was in the act of introducing her to Mr. Green, when he observed that the latter had sunk back upon the sofa, and the last word that he remembered to have heard was, "It is she." After this all was dark and dreary; how long he remained in this condition it was for another to tell. When he awoke he found himself stretched upon the sofa with his boots off, his neckerchief removed, shirt-collar unbuttoned, and his head resting upon a pillow. By his side sat the old man, with the smelling bottle in one hand, and a glass of water in the other, and the little boy standing at the foot of the sofa. As soon as Mr. Green had so far recovered as to be able to speak, he said:

"Where am I, and what does this mean?"

"Wait awhile," replied the old man, "and I will tell you all."

After a lapse of some ten minutes he rose from the sofa, adjusted his apparel, and said:

"I am now ready to hear anything you have to say."

"You were born in America?" said the old man.

"Yes," he replied.

"And you were acquainted with a girl named Mary?" continued the old man.

"Yes, and I loved her as I can love none other."

"That lady whom you met so mysteriously last evening is Mary," replied Mr. Devenant.

George Green was silent, but the fountains of mingled grief and joy stole out from beneath his eyelashes, and glistened like pearls upon his pale and marble-like cheeks. At this juncture the lady again entered the room. Mr. Green sprang from the sofa, and they fell into each other's arms, to the surprise of the old man and little George, and to the amusement of the servants, who had crept up one by one, and were hidden behind the doors or loitering in the hall. When they had given vent to their feelings, they resumed their seats, and each in turn related the adventures through which they had passed.

"How did you find out my name and address?" asked Mr. Green.

"After you had left us in the grave-yard, our little George said, 'O, mamma, if there ain't a book!'

and picked it up and brought it to us. Papa opened it, and said, ' The gentleman's name is written in it, and here is a card of the Hotel de Leon, where I suppose he is stopping.' Papa wished to leave the book, and said it was all a fancy of mine that I had ever seen you before, but I was perfectly convinced that you were my own George Green. Are you married? "

" No, I am not."

" Then, thank God! " exclaimed Mrs. Devenant, for such her name.

The old man, who had been silent all this time, said:

" Now, sir, I must apologize for the trouble you were put to last evening."

" And are you single now? " asked Mr. Green, addressing the lady.

" Yes," she replied.

" This is indeed the Lord's doings," said Mr. Green, at the same time bursting into a flood of tears.

Although Mr. Devenant was past the age when men should think upon matrimonial subjects, yet this scene brought vividly before his eyes the days when he was a young man, and had a wife living, and he thought it was time to call their attention to dinner, which was then waiting. We need scarcely add that Mr. Green and Mrs. Devenant did very little towards diminishing the dinner that day.

After dinner the lovers (for such we have to call them) gave their experience from the time that George Green left the jail, dressed in Mary's clothes.

Up to that time Mr. Green's was substantially as we have related it. Mrs. Devenant's was as follows:

"The night after you left the prison." she said, "I did not shut my eyes in sleep. The next morning, about eight o'clock, Peter, the gardener, came to the jail to see if I had been there the night before, and was informed that I had left a little after dark. About an hour after, Mr. Green came himself, and I need not say that he was much surprised on finding me there, dressed in your clothes. This was the first tidings they had of your escape."

"What did Mr. Green say when he found that I had fled?"

"O" continued Mrs. Devenant, "he said to me when no one was near, 'I hope George will get off, but I fear you will have to suffer in his stead. I told him that if it must be so I was willing to die if you could live."

At this moment George Green burst into tears, threw his arms around her neck, and exclaimed, "I am glad I have waited so long, with the hope of meeting you again."

Mrs. Devenant again resumed her story: "I was kept in jail three days, during which time I was visited by the magistrates and two of the judges. On the third day I was taken out, and master told me that I was liberated upon condition that I be immediately sent out of the State. There happened to be, just at that time, in the neighborhood, a Negro-trader, and he purchased me and I was taken to New

Orleans. On the steamboat we were kept in a close room where slaves are usually confined, so that I saw nothing of the passengers on board, or the towns we passed. We arrived at New Orleans, and were all put in the slave market for sale. I was examined by many persons, but none seemed willing to purchase me; as all thought me too white, and said I would run away and pass as a white woman. On the second day, while in the slave market, and while planters and others were examining slaves and making their purchases, I observed a tall young man with long black hair eyeing me very closely, and then talking to the trader. I felt sure that my time had now come, but the day closed without my being sold. I did not regret this, for I had heard that foreigners made the worst of masters, and I felt confident that the man who eyed me so closely was not an American.

" The next day was the Sabbath. The bells called the people to the different places of worship. Methodists sang, and Baptists immersed, and Presbyterians sprinkled, and Episcopalians read their prayers, while the ministers of the various sects preached that Christ died for all; yet there was some twenty-five or thirty of us poor creatures confined in the ' Negro-Pen,' awaiting the close of the holy Sabbath and the dawn of another day, to be again taken into the market, there to be examined like so many beasts of burden. I need not tell you with what anxiety we waited for the advent of another day.

On Monday we were again brought out, and placed in rows to be inspected; and, fortunately for me, I was sold before we had been on the stand an hour. I was purchased by a gentleman residing in the city, for a waiting-maid for his wife, who was just on the eve of starting for Mobile, to pay a visit to a near relative. I was dressed to suit the situation of a maid-servant; and, upon the whole, I thought that in my new dress I looked as much the lady as my mistress.

"On the passage to Mobile, who should I see, among the passengers, but the tall, long-haired man that had eyed me so closely in the slave market a few day before. His eyes were again on me, and he appeared anxious to speak to me, and I as reluctant to be spoken to. The first evening after leaving New Orleans, soon after twilight had let her curtain down, while I was seated on the deck of the boat, near the ladies' cabin, looking upon the rippled waves, and the reflection of the moon upon the sea, all at onee I saw the tall young man standing by my side. I immediately arose from my seat, and was in the act of returning to the cabin, when he in broken accent said:

"'Stop a moment; I wish to have a word with you. I am your friend.'

"I stopped and looked him full in the face, and he said, 'I saw you some days since in the slave market, and I intended to have purchased you to save you from the condition of a slave. I called on

Monday, but you had been sold and had left the market. I inquired and learned who the purchaser was, and that you had to go to Mobile, so I resolved to follow you. If you are willing I will try and buy you from your present owner, and you shall be free.'

"Although this was said in an honest and off-hand manner, I could not believe the man was sincere in what he said.

"'Why should you wish to set me free?' I asked.

"'I had an only sister,' he replied, 'who died three years ago in France, and you are so much like her that, had I not known of her death, I would most certainly have taken you for her.'

"'However much I may resemble your sister, you are aware that I am not her, and why take so much interest in one whom you have never seen before?'

"'The love,' said he, 'which I had for my sister is transferred to you.'

"I had all along suspected that the man was a knave, and his profession of love confirmed me in my former belief, and I turned away and left him.

"The next day, while standing in the cabin and looking through the window, the French gentleman (for such he was) came to the window, while walking on the guards, and again commenced as on the previous evening. He took from his pocket a bit of paper and put it into my hand, at the same time saying:

"'Take this; it may some day be of service to you. Remember it is from a friend,' and left me instantly.

"I unfolded the paper and found it to be a $100 bank note, on the United States Branch Bank, at Philadelphia. My first impulse was to give it to my mistress, but upon a second thought, I resolved to seek an opportunity, and to return the hundred dollars to the stranger. Therefore I looked for him, but in vain; and had almost given up the idea of seeing him again, when he passed me on the guards of the boat and walked towards the stern of the vessel. It being nearly dark I approached him and offered the money to him.

"He declined, saying at the same time, 'I gave it you—keep it.'

"'I do not want it,' I said.

"'Now,' said he, 'you had better give your consent for me to purchase you, and you shall go with me to France.'

"'But you can not buy me now,' I replied, 'for my master is in New Orleans, and he purchased me not to sell, but to retain in his own family.'

"'Would you rather remain with your present mistress than to be free?'

"'No,' said I.

"'Then fly with me to-night; we shall be in Mobile in two hours from this time, and when the passengers are going on shore, you can take my arm, and you can escape unobserved. The trader who brought you to New Orleans exhibited to me a certificate of your good character, and one from the minister of the church to which you were attached in Virginia; and upon the faith of these assurances, and the love I bear you, I promise before high heaven that I will marry you as soon as it can be done.'

"This solemn promise, coupled with what had already transpired, gave me confidence in the man; and, rash as the act may seem, I determined in an instant to go with him. My mistress had been put under the charge of the captain; and as it would be past ten o'clock when the steamer would land, she accepted an invitation of the captain to remain on board with several other ladies till morning.

"I dressed myself in my best clothes, and put a veil over my face, and was ready on the landing of the boat. Surrounded by a number of passengers, we descended the stage leading to the wharf and were soon lost in the crowd that thronged the quay. As we went on shore we encountered several persons announcing the names of hotels, the starting of boats for the interior, and vessels bound for Europe. Among these was the ship Utica, Captain Pell, bound for Havre.

"'Now,' said Mr. Devenant, this is our chance.'

"The ship was to sail at twelve o'clock that night, at high tide; and following the men who were seeking passengers, we were immediately on board. Devenant told the captain of the ship that I was his sister, and for such we passed during the long voyage. At the hour of twelve the Utica set sail, and we were soon out at sea.

"The morning after we left Mobile, Devenant met me as I came from my state-room and embraced me for the first time. I loved him, but it was only that affection which we have for one who has done us a lasting favor; it was the love of gratitude rather than that of the heart. We were five weeks on the sea, and yet the passage did not seem long, for Devenant was so kind. On our arrival at Havre, we were married and came to Dunkirk, and I have resided here ever since."

At the close of this narrative, the clock struck ten, when the old man, who was accustomed to retire at an early hour, rose to take leave, saying at the same time:

"I hope you will remain with us to-night."

Mr. Green would fain have excused himself, on the ground that they would expect him and wait at the hotel, but a look from the lady told him to accept the invitation. The old man was the father of Mrs. Devenant's deceased husband, as you will no doubt long since have supposed.

A fortnight from the day on which they met in the grave-yard Mr. Green and Mrs. Devenant were joined in holy wedlock; so that George and Mary, who had loved each other so ardently in their younger days, were now husband and wife.

A celebrated writer has justly said of women: "A woman's whole life is a history of affections. The heart is her world; it is there her ambition strives for empire; it is there her avarice seeks for hidden treasures. She sends forth her sympathies on adventure; she embarks her whole soul in the traffic of affection; and if shipwrecked, her case is hopeless, for it is bankruptcy of the heart."

Mary had ever reason to believe that she would never see George again; and although she confessed that the love she bore him was never transferred to her first husband, we can scarcely find fault with her for marrying Mr. Devenant. But the adherence of George Green to the resolution never to marry, unless to his Mary, is, indeed, a rare instance of the fidelity of man in the matter of love. We can but blush for our country's shame, when we call to mind the fact, that while George and Mary Green, and numbers of other fugitives from American slavery, could receive protection from any of the governments of Europe, they could not in safety return to their own land until countless treasure, untold suffering and anguish, and the life blood of half a million men, had been paid as the price of the bondman's chain.

CHAPTER V.

HOW SOL. JONES WAS LEFT.

I.

DURING the decade of the thirties, and for years afterward, there resided on an affluent of the Rappahannock, in Culpepper county, Virginia, one Solomon Jones. Mr. Jones was the inheritor of an estate with all that term would imply fifty years ago in the "Old Dominion"—numerous slaves, the F. F. V. idea of domination of race, and those false conceptions of right begotten of "chattel" ownership. Though naturally possessed of many excellent traits of character, he was harsh and unrelenting towards those who sustained to him the relation of property.

On the little stream running through his domain he had erected a grist mill for his own accommodation and the profit to be derived therefrom in doing the work of his neighbors, and in supplying adjacent towns with the product of his mill; for Solomon had business tact and push far beyond his surroundings and time.

The business of distributing his merchandise was entrusted to a mulatto named Sam, who traveled far and near in the discharge of his duties, and being a shrewd, intelligent fellow, was enabled to pick up much valuable information relative to the ways of the outside world.

The estate also possessed a blacksmith in the person of a stalwart negro, Peter, who rejoiced in no drop of Caucassian blood. The wife of each of these men was respectively the sister of the other, but Dinah, the wife of Sam, for some reason history has not recorded, was a free woman, and both families were childless. This fact was not at all pleasing to the owner of the plantation, and became the source of much annoyance and abuse as the master saw less and less prospect of replenishing his coffers from the sale or labor of a second generation.

Stung by the continued upbraidings and base advances of "Old Sol," as Jones ultimately came to be called, the two families began seriously to discuss the propriety of *emigrating* Northward. The knowledge picked up by Sam now became available. He had heard much in his journeyings of the methods of escape, and the courses pursued, and having unlimited control of the teams about the mill and a general acquaintance for miles away was, consequently, deemed the proper person to direct the escape. Acting upon his advice the women quietly laid in such a stock of provisions as would suffice them for several days, together with so much of clothing as was deemed indispensible. Thus equipped, one Saturday night, in July, 1843, the men saddled two of the best horses on the plantation and with their wives mounted behind them set out and by daylight were far away among the mountains to the northwestward. A halt was made for the day in a secluded ravine where some pasturage was found, and again at night they pushed vigorously on, putting two nights of fleet travel between them and the plantation before their flight was discovered, as the master and family were absent and none other had thought of inquiring into their whereabouts.

On returning to his home on Monday, Mr. Jones learned of the absence of Peter from the smithy, Sam from his accustomed duties and the women from the cabins, and the conviction flashed upon him that he was minus three valuable pieces of property, and when the disappearance of his best horses was ascertained, his wrath knew no bounds. A plan of search was instituted, but before it was thoroughly organized, two or three more days had elapsed.

Meanwhile, the fugitives were making their way rapidly towards the Ohio river which they crossed with little difficulty a short distance below Wheeling, and were soon threading the hill country of Southeastern Ohio. Arriving in Harrison county after the lapse of some twenty days, they thought they might safely betake themselves to the more public highway and to daylight. Here was their mistake, for on the first day of this public exhibition of confidence, when a few miles north of Cadiz, they looked back and a short distance in the rear beheld "Ol' Massa" and two or three men in pursuit. They betook themselves to the adjacent woods and all but Sam succeeded in escaping. He, poor fellow, was captured and lodged in jail at Cadiz whilst the pursuit of the others was continued, but in vain; for avoiding every human habitation and moving only under cover of night they pushed forward and reached the home of a Mr. Williams, a Quaker, residing near Massillon, where Sam's wife learned of his capture, and bidding good-bye to the others, retraced her foot-steps slowly to her Virginian home, expecting to find her husband. Not so however.

II.

Immediately a portion of the people of Cadiz found a slave had been incarcerated in the jail for safe keeping, whilst the master was in search of others, they sued out a writ of *habeas corpus*, and there being none to appear against the prisoner or show cause why he should not be released, he was soon set at liberty by the judge. Grown wiser by experience, he betook himself to the cover of forests, secluded pathways and darkness and all trace of him was soon lost.

After a vain search for the others, Mr. Jones returned to Cadiz only to find that the official cage had been opened and that his bird was flown. His imprecations upon the devoted town were terrible, but no damage was done farther than shocking moral and religious sensibilities, and when the ebulitions of his wrath had somewhat subsided he returned home, where in a few days he was accosted by Sam's faithful Dinah, whom he most impiously rebuffed when she inquired as to the whereabouts of her husband.

III.

Infused with the hope of making a fortune out of the Morus morticaulus speculation which spread as a craze over the country during the later years of the decade, there came to Massillon, from the east, in 1837, Cyrus Ford, a man of progressive ideas, who soon associated himself with the Quakers of the neighborhood in acts of underground philanthropy. His hopes with regard to mulberry riches failed, but his fears with respect to the ague was more than realized, as he imbibed the dense malarial exhalations arising from the Tuscarawas to such an extent as to shake him in his boots, and in 1841 he abandoned the valley and settled himself on a purchase east of what was then known as "Doan's Corners," now East Cleveland, a short distance from where Adelbert College stands. For years he resided in an unpretentious house situated just in front of the site of the present hospitable home of his son, Horace Ford, Esq., Euclid Avenue.

One September morning, in 1843, young Horace had been started early after the cows, but scarcely had he left the door when, in the early dawn, he was hailed from the roadside. Approaching the caller he found standing at the gateway the Williams

HOW SOL. JONES WAS LEFT. 129

turn-out from Massillon, and on the box the old gentleman's son Ed, a young man about his own age.

"What's up, Ed?" said young Ford.

"Not much. Don't thee see the curtains are down?" was the reply.

"O, ah, I see."

"Not exactly thee don't, for them curtains are opeque, but there are two persons within for whom, as we believe, search is now being made in town yonder. Massillon was thoroughly searched, and it was not until last evening we dared to start out. Thee and thy father must now provide for the poor beings and see them off to the Queen's Dominion."

Without further ceremony Peter Jones and Mary, his wife, were bidden to alight and in a few minutes were safely secreted on the premises of Mr. Ford.

IV.

On Seneca street, in that early day, near the present site of the criminal court rooms stood John Bell's barber-shop, the more euphoneous term, "tonsorial parlors," being then all unknown. John was a sterling, wide awake darkie, and for years one of the *principal forwarding agents* in the growing city. To him during the day young Ford applied for transportation for the arrival of the morning, but was informed that matters were entirely too hot to undertake their shipment at that time, but that he should wait until the third evening and then bring them in promptly at nine o'clock and he would have everything ready for their transfer. They were taken into the city in accordance with this arrangement and in thirty minutes were out on the blue waters of Erie duly headed for Canada.

Scarcely three weeks had elapsed when the William's establishment again stood at the gate of Mr. Ford, this time having brought Sam who had succeeded after weary watchings in reaching the Quaker settlement at Massillon. He was anxious to tarry and wait the coming of his wife, who he thought could be duly appraised of his whereabouts by letter. To this end he gave young Horace the name of a friend to whom he could safely write and inform her of his escape from jail and safe arrival at the lake. Dr. Edwin Cowles, Jarvis F. Hanks and Cornelius Coakly were called in to advise in the matter and it was unanimously agreed that Sam should go forward, and if his wife could be found she was to be sent to him as soon as possible. In accordance with this decision Sam went to Canada, but much to the surprise of Mr. Ford returned in about three weeks, almost frantic for the recovery of his wife. A second letter was written, advising the unknown friend of Sam's whereabouts.

Awaiting an answer, Sam went to work for Mr. Ford chopping upon the sloping hillside a short distance west of the site of the Garfield Monument. He had been engaged thus about a month when the Williams carriage again drove up, this time bringing

HOW SOL. JONES WAS LEFT.

Dinah, whose meeting with her husband was of a most emotional character, manifested in shouts and praises and thanksgiving to God, and choicest blessings called down upon the head of Horace whose second epistle had reach its destination, on receipt of which she had immediately set out on her long journey to join him. In a day or two the twain were forwarded to Canada. Immediately on their departure, the junior Ford mailed the following:

CLEVELAND, O., Dec. —, 1843.

Solomon Jones, Esq.

Dear Sir :—I have seen your chattels, Pete, Mary and Sam, safe off for Canada. If I can serve you any farther, I am at your command. Truly,——————— "

CHAPTER VI.

EDWARD HOWARD.

I.

"I SAY, Ed, if you get away with me, it will have to be done soon."

" Yes, Massa Coppoc; da's 'ginnin' to spishun you right smart."

" I know that, Ed, and if you are ready to strike for freedom to-night, we will see what can be done. If not, I must be off."

" Well, Massa, dis chil' am ready. Him no lan' to sell, no truck to 'spose of, no wife an' chil'n to 'cupy his detention, an' he 'queaths his 'sitiashun to any one wat wants it."

" Very well, Ed, as soon as all is quiet, meet me at the shed in your Sunday best; and now be off."

" Suah, sartin, bof, Massa Coppoc."

The above conversation took place about twenty miles back from Ohio between a young Buckeye who was ostensibly vending some kind of wares among the F. F. V's., but really paving the way to that startling episode at Harper's Ferry, in which he, a few years later, played so conspicuous a part; and a genuine descendant of Ham, after the real Virginian type, quaint, ungainly, and standing about six feet six, and rejoicing in the sobriquet, Ed. Howard.

Coppoc had been some little time in the neighborhood, and the impression began to prevail that his presence boded no guaranty of the retention of movavle property. This his shrewd eye had perceived, and his resolve to rescue Ed. led to the above conversation, the conclusion of a series that had transpired between them.

II.

Eleven o'clock came, and with it a *black cloud*, which completely cut off all sight of the twinkling stars from a man who stood pensively listening, beneath an old shed that stood back on the plantation, and from the cloud, " a still small voice saying:" "Is you heah, Massa Coppoc?"

"Here, Ed., and now follow me without a word," saying which he led the way to a pasture field where two fleet horses were soon bridled and saddled, and the two men rode deliberately away. Once out of the neighborhood their speed was quickened, and long before daybreak the horses were turned loose a short distance out from Wheeling. Entering the city they proceeded directly to the wharf, where a boat was found just leaving for Pittsburgh. On this they took passage, as master and servant, for Wellsville.

Once in the latter place, Ed. was consigned to the shipping department of the *Road*, and young Coppoc hastened to his home, near Salem, conscious that confusion would likely follow as a result of last night's ride.

III.

Daylight crept slowly over the Virginian hills, and when it was ascertained that Ed. and the two best horses were gone, there was a commotion indeed. A rally was at once made, and dogs and men put upon the track, and about noon the horses were found near where they had been turned loose, but no trace of the fugitives could be obtained for some little time, owing to the hour in which they took the boat, but at length some one reported having seen two such persons take the night packet up the river. Taking advantage of the first steamer up, Ed's master hastened to Pittsburgh, where he learned of the debarkation of his *property*, and returned to Wellsville on the first boat.

In the meantime there had come down from the immediate vicinity of Salem, a Mr. Pennock, a blacksmith, the owner of a small farm. Going to the river town several times in the year for his supplies, Mr. Pennock had fitted a long close box, opening in the rear, to his "running gears" and in this the bars of iron were thrust, frequently of such length as to project several feet.

Now it so happened that the day after Ed. was left in Wellsville, Mr. Pennock went in for a supply of iron. When he had made his purchase and was about to return to his hotel, the dealer, who like Mr.

Pennock, was an underground man, said, "See here. Pennock, I've a *soft bar* about six feet and a half long, I'd like to send up to Bonsall."

"How much does it weigh?"

"About one sixty, I'd judge."

"That will make me a deal of a load, besides I don't see how it can be done."

"You can leave that to me."

"Where is it; I'd like to see how it looks."

"No, that will not do. It is in Excelsior Station and the probabilities are there will be vigorous efforts made to recapture it, so you must 'eyes off.' If you undertake the carrying I will see to the rest."

"All right."

That night there was made a little readjustment of the wagon box, some hay and a blanket were placed on top of the projecting bars and there, extended at full length, was the form of Edward Howard, when in the early morning Mr. Pennock was ready to depart.

Meanwhile his master had procured from a Virginia friend, a couple of good horses and himself as an assistant, and entered Wellsville on the morning of Mr. Pennock's departure. After a half day's fruitless search with the aid of an officer, they became satisfied that the object of their regard had been forwarded, so they took the road north. Overtaking the old blacksmith with his iron rattling along, they enquired, "Have you seen any nigger along the road?"

"What kind of a one was he?"

"Why a black one with a wholly head, tall and slim like a d—d yankee bean pole."

"Well, gentlemen, I haven't seen no such a one, indeed I have seen none at all."

"Well, have you heard of any?"

"I've not heard the word nigger since I left home, two days ago, until now."

"Where are you from?"

"Salem, and like enough you'll find him there, for they say them Bonsalls keeps a power of runaways."

"Well, we're going up to see. Good day, sir."

"Good day, gentleman," and each party pursued its way.

That night Pennock stayed at the "Old Buckeye House," New Lisbon, the wagon was run into the barn, and at a proper hour the "soft bar" was taken out and placed in the hay-mow, "to prevent rust," as the blacksmith facetiously remarked to his friend Boniface. The next day on arriving home, he learned his interlocutors had preceded him some hours, and were registered at one of the taverns as cattle buyers or drovers rather, where young Coppoc had caught a glimpse of them, and informed his friends of their real character.

On the morrow the pseudo dealers called on a neighboring farmer and desired to be introduced among the best stock raisers of the vicinity.

"Thee had better be leaving these parts, gentlemen,"

said the honest Quaker, to whom the appeal was made. "If thee knows when thee is well off, for thy errand is understood, and thee will have the Coppocs and the Bonsalls down on thee in an hour, and I could not assure thy lives for a moment when they come."

There was no parly, but two horses were headed southward, and none too soon, for in a short time half a dozen young men armed to the teeth, rode up and inquired for the strangers. When informed of their departure they started in pursuit. Then began one of the most exciting races ever witnessed in Columbian county. The pursued had smelled mischief in the air, and away they flew, and after them the pursuers, dashing over hill and across valley, occasionally catching glimpses of each other, until the whole distance to the Ohio was passed. Reaching Gardiner's Ferry, at East Liverpool, the Southerners put their jaded horses aboard the boat and were soon on the sacred soil of Virginia. When Gardiner returned the other party was in waiting, but reluctantly took his advice to remain on the soil of their native state.

IV.

All apprehension of immediate danger removed, Ed., who, by the advice of Coppoc, assumed the name "Sam," remained quietly at Mr. Pennock's for some time, in fact, made it his headquarters for the winter, working for his board and doing odd jobs, from the proceeds of which he purchased some clothes and a long smooth-bore rifle, of which he was passionately fond, and with which he practiced much, often repeating, " I shall put a hole through the man suah, who comes to claim that 'wa'd," for the whole region from the river to the lake had been flooded with bills minutely describing him and offering $500 for his apprehension.

When spring fairly opened he made up his mind to seek the Queen's Dominion as rapidly as possible, and accordingly packed his few effects in a bandana, threw " 'Tection," as he called his smooth-bore, across his shoulder, and proceeded cautiously northward.

Arriving at Warren, he sought the home of a colored family that had been pointed out to him as a safe retreat. Approaching the door, he heard a number of voices, which he recognized by the melody as being of his kind, singing with great gusto:

> " Matthew's saint
> Without putty or paint,
> And Joel's a prophet, we know it;
> Whatever they say
> Don't refuse to obey,
> But shut up your eyes and go it,"

words perpetrated by one John Morley on two distinguished local politicians of the Democratic persuasion of the period of '56, and very popular as part of a campaign song.

Fully assured by the style of the singing, Sam, the

only name he now recognized, made his presence known and was cordially received by the colored brethren present, among them the *distinguished* tonsorial artist, Prof. A. L. C. Day, and Benjamin F. Scott, familiarly known as "Old Ben," a darkey whose cupidity and avarice knew no bounds. Recognizing in Sam, as he believed, the Edward Howard of the handbill, he began planning for the reward.

Ascertaining what was up, Dr. D. B. Woods and Postmaster Webb, two sterling Democrats, got possession of Sam and took him to a by-road about two miles out of town, where they enjoined him to keep away from the more public highways and proceed about twenty miles north where he would find a colored man named Jenkins, in whom he could rely.

Whilst the doctor and his friend were thus humanely engaged, the colored brethren of Warren took Old Ebony out of town and so severely flogged him that his back prasented the appearance of a genuine plantation administration. Determined to realize something for his time and pains, the old sinner proceeded to the northern part of the county and palmed himself off as a genuine fugitive, and so adroitely did he play the role as to secure twelve or fifteen dollars before the counterfeit was detected.

As for Sam, he took the advice of his Democratic deliverers, and in due time found himself under the hospitable roof of "Nigger" Jenkins, as he was more commonly called, residing in the township of Mesopotania, and by him was forwarded to the home of Joseph Tinan, near the centre of Rome.

"Uncle Joe" was a famous agent in his day. Tall and imposing in appearance, and of more than ordinary intelligence, he commanded universal respect, and so pronounced were his opinions on the curse of slavery that his home had long been recognized as "Old Reliable Station." By him Sam was cordially received, and his *arm* carefully inspected. Then the old gentleman would have Sam make an exhibition of his skill as a marksman. So well did the efforts of his temporary ward please him, that Uncle Joe was constrained to show him the armory of the "Black String Band," an organization that had then but recently sprung into existence and having for its more immediate object the protection of John Brown, should his arrest be attempted. The distinctive badge of this band was a small black cord, used instead of a button in fastening the shirt collar. Hence the name.

The sight of the glittering barrels made Sam's eyes fairly dance with delight, and he exclaimed, "Massa Coppoc say thay's gwine to be wah an' de cullud pussons will all be free."

"O no, Sam, there's going to be no war. These guns are for another purpose."

Little did Uncle Joe, well as he was posted, know of the ultimate plans of Old Ossawattomie. His dusky visitor was even a little in advance of him with regard to what was already fomenting in Dixie.

In the northwest part of Andover, Ohio, resides an old patriarch, Jehaziel Carpenter, familiarly known as "the Deacon," now numbering his over ninety summers. For over sixty years he has tenanted on the same farm, and his home has ever been one of the broadest hospitality, and to none more so than to the panting fugitive. Just a little way off stands the rather tall, old-fashioned country house of his former neighbor, Garlic, whose language never betrayed the fact that he had any official church relation. In fact we think his name, significant as it was, had no place on the muster roll of the church militant, and yet he was *game* in many a hard fight for truth and righteousness.

V.

Cleveland and vicinity was flooded with circulars, advertising a man, wife and child, who had been traced to that city, and offering a large reward for their delivery to the reputed owner. Friend and foe were alike on the lookout. Efforts were making by the one to secure them a passage across the lake, whilst the other was as assiduously watching every vessel to prevent their escape.

Thus matters stood when the man, Martin by name, looking out of an upper window, espied his master among the passers by on Water street. This being communicated to those who had them in charge, it was at once determined the family should not be shipped by lake.

That night, when all was quiet and still, a close carriage passed out Pittsburgh street, and before daylight

Martin and his wife were in safe quarters near Chagrin Falls. Thence they were taken the next night to the home of Mr. Cook, in Middlefield, and as rapidly transmitted by him to a pious old deacon's in Gustavus.

VI.

Night had settled down over village and farm house; Deacon Jehaziel's evening prayers had been said and he was quietly dreaming of the time

"When you and I were young, Maggie,"

and Garlic, just returned from Jefferson, had turned his horse into the pasture, when up to the door of each came a vehicle. Garlic at once recognized the horse of the old Baptist Boanerges, Tinan, from Rome, whilst the deacon was aroused by the quieter voice of his Congregational brother from Gustavus. What transpired from this time until the city of Erie was reached is buried in the tombs of Garlic, a Hayward, a Gould and a Drury.

VII.

In the township of Harbor Creek, Pa., east of the city of Erie, and a short distance out of Wesleyville, was the farm house of Frank Henry, a man of medium size, black hair, eyes of the same hue and sparkling like diamonds, nervous temperament, quick, wiry and the soul of honor and generosity. For a young man he was one of the best known and most efficient conductor-agents in Western Pennsylvania. About mid-summer, 1858, he received the following note:—

EDWARD HOWARD.

Erie, Pa., 51, 7, 5881.

Dear Frank:

The mirage lifts Long Point into view. Oooo. Come up and see the beautiful sight. I can't promise a view to-morrow.   Truly,

Jehiel Towner.

That evening found Mr. Henry early in the presence of Mr. Towner, inquiring diligently as to the great *natural* phenomenon which had brought the land of the Canucks so distinctly to view.

"Yes, yes, it became visible last night about twelve o'clock, when Drury's team came in from Girard bearing three fugitives. They are down in the "Retreat Himrod," and must be put across the lake in the shortest and safest possible manner, for parties in town are on the lookout for them, as all are liberally advertised. I believe you are just the man to undertake the transportation. Will you do it?"

"Are they to go from the 'Retreat,' as usual?"

"Not as usual. So close a watch is kept for them that it is thought best to send them off and have them shipped from some point along the beach."

"There's a big risk, Towner."

"Yes, a chance to pay a thousand dollars and see the inside of the 'Western' without charge. But you know you are to have nothing to do with runaway niggers. I will just send you some 'passengers' to forward. Shall they be sent?"

"I shrink from no humanitarian work. Let them come."

A few preliminaries were settled and the parties separated. The next night Hamilton Waters, a nearly blind mulatto, long a resident of Erie, guided by a little boy, drove into Mr. Henry's yard and unloaded a cargo which the receiver thus describes:

"The old man brought me three of the strangest looking passengers you ever saw. I can, to-day, remember how oddly they looked as they clambered out of the wagon. There was a man they called Sam, a great strapping fellow, something over thirty years old, I should say. He was loose jointed, with a head like a pumpkin and a mouth like a cavern, its vast circumference always stretched in a glorious grin; for no matter how bad Sam might feel, the grin had so grown into his black face that it never vanished. I remember how, a few nights after, when the poor fellow was scared just about out of his wits, that his grin, though a little ghastly, was as broad as ever. Sam was one of the queerest characters I ever met. His long arms seemed like wrists, his long legs all ankles; and when he walked his nether limbs had a flail-like flop that made him look like a runaway windmill. The bases upon which rested this fearfully and wonderfully made superstructure were abundantly ample. Unlike the forlorn hope who

'One stocking on one foot he had,
The other on a shoe,'

he on one foot wore an old shoe—at least a number twelve—and on the other an enormously heavy boot, and his trouser-legs, by a grim fatility, were similarly unbalanced, for while the one was tucked in the boot-top, its fellow, from knee down, had wholly vanished. Sam wore a weather-beaten and brimless 'tile' on his head, and carried an old-fashioned, long-barrelled rifle. He set great store by his 'ole smooth bo',' though he handled it in a gingerly kind of a way that suggested a greater fear of its kicks than confidence in its aim.

Sam's companions were an intelligent-looking negro about twenty-five, named Martin, and his wife, a pretty quadroon girl with thin lips and a pleasant voice, for all the world like Eliza in Uncle Tom's Cabin. She carried a plump little picanniny on her breast, over which a shawl was slightly drawn. She was an uncommonly attractive young woman, and I made up my mind then and there that she shouldn't be carried back to slavery if I could help it.

As there was close pursuit, station "Sanctum Sanctorum" was again called into requisition, though as it was summer, no draft was made on the church wood-pile. Here they were kept for several days, none knowing of their whereabouts except two intimate friends of Mr. Henry, whose house being under nightly espionage necessitated their assistance.

Through Wesleyville runs a little stream, Fourmile Creek, to the lake, and nearly parallel to it a public highway. From the mouth of this creek it was proposed to ship the fugitives to Long Point, Canada, a distance of some thirty-five or forty miles, but for some days the wind was unfavorable. At length one dark and stormy night Mr. Henry received notice that the wind was favorable and a boat in readiness.

What was to be done? It would not do for him to take anything from his house, that would excite suspicion; the same would be true if he went to the houses of his friends. Bethinking himself of an honest Jacksonian Democrat, a man with a generous heart, residing about half way down to the lake, he decided to take a venture. Proceeding to the old church he formed the little party in single file and marched them through the rain to the door of this man, familiarly known as "General" Kilpatrick, a man of giant proportions, and afterwards sheriff of Erie county.

Rap, rap, rap, went the knuckels of the leader against the door, which soon stood wide ajar, revealing the proprietor with a thousand interrogation points freezing into his face that July night, as he paused for a moment, one hand holding aloft a candle whilst the other shaded his eyes as he peered out upon the wet and shivering crowd gathered about his doorway, the very picture of dumfounded astonishment. The situation was soon grasped; he hustled the party into the house, gave the door a significant slam and in a pious air that would have startled even Peter Cartwright, exclaimed, "Henry, what in hell does this mean?."

"It means," General, replied Mr. Henry, "these

are a party of fugitives from slavery I am about sending to Canada; they are destitute, as you can see, and closely pursued; their only crime is a desire for freedom; that young woman and mother has been sold from her husband and child to a dealer in the far South for the vilest of purposes, and if recaptured will be consigned to a life of shame."

Meanwhile the woman's eyes were pleading eloquently, whilst a dubious grin overspread the entire of Sam's ebony phiz, and the host looked assumedly fierce and angry as he retorted " Well, what the d—l do you want of me?"

" Clothing and provisions."

"You do, do you?" came back in tones even gruffer than before. " See here you darkies, this is a bad job. Canada is full of runaway niggers already. They're a-freezin' and a-starvin' by thousands. Why, I was over there t'other day, and saw six niggers dead by the roadside. More'n forty were strung up in the trees with the crows feedin' on their black carcasses," and turning to Sam, " *You* better go back, d'ye *hear!* They'll make your black hide into razor strops 'nless than a week. I paid a dollar for one made from a black nigger. They're sending hundreds of them across the sea every week."

During this harangue, Sam was shaking in his footgear and his eyes rolled widely on the background of that inexpressible grin. His fingers clutched convulsively his shooting-iron, and he evidently didn't know which to do, turn it upon his

Democratic entertainer or keep his "powder dry" for Canuck crows. The woman caught, through this assumed roughness, the inner heart of the man, and though she shuddered at the pictures drawn, and the possibilities of a grave in the lake, yet she preferred that, or even to be food for the vultures of Canada, to return to an ignominious servitude.

Then came a strange medley: Blanket and hood —"there, the huzzy"—a basket of provisions— "d—m me if I'll ever help a set of runaway niggers, no sir, it's agin my religion"—off came his own coat and was hurled at the astonished Sam with, "There you black imp, you'll find 'em on the Pint waitin' for ye; they'll catch ye and kill ye and skin yer carcass for a scare-crow and take yer hide for a drum head, and play 'God save the Queen' with your bones. Yes, sir, I shall see them long shanks converted into drum-sticks the next time I go over."

All else being done, he thrust his hands into his pockets and drawing thence a quantity of change bestowed it upon the woman, exclaiming, "There, take that; it will help bury the baby, if you will go. Better go back, you huzzy; better go back."

Everything ready, the party was shoved out, but as he passed over the threshold, Sam's tongue was loosened, and with the smile all the time deepening, and the great tears rolling down his sable cheeks, he broke forth:

"Look 'e hyar, Massa, you's good to we uns, an' fo' de Lo'd I tank you. Ef enny No'then gemmen

EDWARD HOWARD.

hankah fur my chances in the Souf I'zins in favor ob de same. For de good Lo'd, I tank you, I do *suah.*"

"Hist, you black rascal." said the man in the doorway, "And see here, Henry, remember you never were at my house with a lot of damned niggers in the night. Do you understand?"

"All right, sir. No man will ever charge you with abolitionism. If he does, call on me. I can swear you denounce it in most unmeasured terms."

The rain had now ceased; the stars were out and the party trudged rapidly down to the lake, caring little for the mud and wet. The boat was found in waiting, and Martin and his wife had just waded out to it when Henry and Sam, standing on the shore, had their attention attracted by a noise, as the crushing of a fence-board, and looking to the westward they saw a man sliding down the bank into the shadow. Old "'tection" was immediately brought to aim, so exact that had Henry not struck the barrel upward just as the trigger was pulled, sending the ball whistling in the air, there could not have failed a subject for a "first-class funeral." The sneak took to his heels, Sam took to the boat, and Henry stood long upon the shore peering into the darkness, catching the rich, mellow tones of Mrs. Martin's voice as she warbled forth in real negro minstrelsy, interrupted by an occasional "'lujah" from Sam as the boat receded,

"There is a railrod undergroun'
  On which de negroes lope,
An' when dey gets dare ticket
  Dare hearts is full ob hope;
De engine nebber whistles
  An' de cars dey make no noise,
But dey carry off de darkies,
  Dare wives, an' girls, an' boys."

Returning homeward, Mr. Henry traced the human sleuth-hound by his footsteps in the mud, the nibbling of his horses where they had been left, and the marks of his carriage wheels at Wesleyville where they turned toward Erie, and were lost in the new made tracks of the early morning marketers.

VIII.

Time passed; the years of the war came and went; peace smiled upon the country; John Brown and young Coppoc slept beneath sodded mounds, whilst the soul of the former went " marching on," and the genial, generous Henry was keeping the lighthouse on the eastern extremity of Presque Isle, at the entrance of Erie harbor or bay. Going over to the city one day he received a letter bearing the Dominion post mark. It was without date, and with some difficulty he deciphered the following:

Dere Ser, Mistur Henri:

I'ze glad ter bee abul to rite ye. I'ze dun wel sens dat nite. I'ze got a wife an' chilin'. De lor sen me into de ile kentry bress him and Sam make sum muni. I sen to yer a draf for 100 dollars gib fift to de men in de bote an' kepe 50 fo' buks fo' you one selfe tel de kros man Sam feah no kro 'oz no razr strap, tank de lor.

>Your lubbin fren Sam,
>>wo wuz EDWUD HOWUD.

CHAPTER VII.

PLUCKY CHARLEY.

I.

"CHA'LEY, I say Cha'ley, a' my chil'ns gone 'cept you, and Massa's done gone an' sol' you, and I'll nebber see you 'gin in a' dis bressed wu'l', nebber! nebber!"

"Guess not, mudder; ol' Massa promised you when he put de udders in de coffle to keep me allus."

"Yes, Cha'ley, dat am so, but dis bery mornin' I hear 'im tell dat unspec'ble trader he'll sen' you to him Monday mornin' shu'ah, an' dat he mus' put yer in jail till he start de drove fur down de riber. May de Lor' help yer my chil' when yer ol' mudder's ha't am clean broke."

"De Lor' help you, mudder; dis chil' help hisself, so jus' gib me my dinnah, mudder, fo' I mus go to de fiel' to do Massa's arran' to de boss."

Had the ear of the reader been present in the little back kitchen of a fine plantation residence in Loudon county, Virginia, in the autumn of 1855, the above conversation might have been heard between a colored woman rather past middle life and her son, an athletic young man of about twenty years of age,

PLUCKY CHARLEY.

as they conversed in low tones. The woman had long been the cook in the family and had lived to see her husband and all her children except Charley, the youngest, sold for the southern market, joined in the coffle like so many beasts and driven away.

To alleviate her agony, she had been promised that Charley should ever remain with her, and resting in this promise she had toiled unrepiningly on, whilst the growing lad had been kept as a kind of boy-of-all chores about the house, going occasionally, as a kind of body servant with his master to Washington, Baltimore and Wheeling, thus being enabled, by close observation, to pick up a little general knowledge.

Thus things nad passed until the morning of the day in question, when she accidently overheard the sale of the boy, and with an aching heart communicated the news to him as he came to the kitchen as usual for his dinner. How earnestly her mother's heart may have prayed that the Lord would open up a way of escape for her darling boy no one can tell, neither does it matter, for no sooner was the fact of the sale communicated to him than the mental resolve of the youth was taken to effect an escape.

The frugal dinner was dispatched in silence, the mission to the field duly executed and a prompt return thereof made, much to the satisfaction of the master.

II.

Night, sable goddess, had spread her curtain over earth, and the valleys amid the Alleghenies were sleeping in quiet, when Charley, crawling from his couch, so stealthily, indeed, as not to disturb the early slumbers of his mother, crept softly to the stable, saddled his master's best steed, noiselessly led it to the public highway beyond the mansion, and, turning its head toward the realm of freedom, mounted, and giving the noble beast the rein, was soon moving with such velocity as to place fifty miles between him and his master and mother by the time the first gray tinge of morning began to break along the eastern hills. Riding deep into a wooded ravine he secured the horse for the day, and then betook himself to sleep. At evening he unloosed the beast stripping it of saddle and bridle, and then betook himself to the woods and by-ways, shunning all towns and subsisting on green corn and such fruits as he could find for a period of fifteen days, when, weary and forlorn, he entered Wheeling just before daylight. An utter stranger, and almost perishing with hunger, he knew not what to do, but seeing a light in the bar-room of the City Hotel he resolved to enter, hoping to find some attendant of his own race, to whom he could appeal for food and assistance across the river. Instead of an attaché, the landlord was himself already astir. Though residing on sacred soil and in many respects a typical

PLUCKY CHARLEY.

Virginian, mine host kept only hired servants, and though in no wise disposed to discuss the merits of the peculiar institution pro or con, he was often able to make wise suggestions to the thoughtless or inconsiderate of both sections who might temporarily be his guests.

Once fairly within and under the scrutinizing gaze of this man, Charley made bold to ask for bread.

"Bread, you want, do you, you black runaway?" said the landlord rather roughly.

"I'ze no runa—"

"Yes you are you black rascal. Come go with me and I'll show you something.

Instinctively following the footsteps of the landlord, Charley was led to the stable where he recognized at once his master's horse. Then the man took a paper from his pocket and read a complete description of him, and closed by saying: "You are this Charley and your master will give $500 to any man who will return you."

Seeing he was caught, Charley pleaded, "O Lor,' Massa, doan gib me up."

"No, I'll not; your master is close at hand. Do you see that house across the lot yonder?"

"Yes, Massa, I sees."

"Well, you go there quick. Tell them I sent you and that they must take care of you. Go right in at the back door. Be quick or you'll be caught."

With both heart and feet a-bound, Charley made for the designated place. He found only a woman, sick upon her bed. Ere he had fairly made his errand known, there was heard the sound of horses' feet upon the street, and looking out, Charley saw his master and another man coming at full speed, and began to cry.

"Get under the bed, quick, and keep perfectly still," said the woman; a command which was obeyed without questioning. Catching up her baby, the woman gave it a tumble which set it to crying like mad. Just then the master thrust his head in at the door and inquired, "Have you seen a young nigger come in here?"

"Hush h-u!" "Wah ka-wa!" "What did!" "Wha-ka wa wa!" "hush there—did you say?" "Ka-wha wa wah."

"I say did"—"ka wha ka wha wa!" "did you see a young nigger come in here?"

"We wha ke wah wa!" "hush-t-h-e-re!"—"husband is"—"we wa wah!"—"at the barn!"—"we wa ah!"—"he can tell you!"—"wa we wah ke wha!" and the door was slammed to by the disgusted Southeron.

Whilst the trio were hastening to the barn, Charley, in obedience to the woman's directions, hastily ascended a ladder in the corner of the room, which he drew up, and placed a board in such a way as to obliterate all appearance of an opening in the floor.

The conference at the barn was short, and away went the riders up the road in hot pursuit of a mythical nigger the man at the barn had seen running in that direction not half an hour before.

In a few minutes the husband returned to the house, milk pail in hand, but entirely ignorant of what had transpired within. "What about the boy, wife, those men were enquiring about? I supposed they were in pursuit of some one, so I sent them up the road after an imaginary man," he said.

"Well, I don't know anything about your imaginary man, but I know about the boy," replied the wife.

"Well, where is he?"

"He went from under my bed up the ladder whilst the men were going for you. Baby helped the matter mightily. Now you must carry the poor fellow something to eat."

As soon as it was deemed safe, the ladder was let down, and Charley was supplied with a hearty breakfast, and then bidden to make himself comfortable for the day, a thing he was not slow to do, as he had slept little since his flight began. When evening came, he was called down, and after a bountiful supper, which was dispatched in silence, he was taken to the road where three horses were standing. On one of these a man was already seated; the second Charley was bidden to mount, and into the saddle of the third his kind host vaulted.

Moving around the town, they came to a road leading northward, Charley's feelings alternately ebbing and flowing between fear and hope, for, notwithstanding the kindness of his host and hostess, he could but fear that he was to be given up for the $500.

Proceeding some distance up the river, the horses were hitched in some bushes and the party descended to the river, where a boat was loosened and Charley was bidden to enter. When all were seated, the little craft pushed out into the stream, and soon Charley and his host stepped onto the other shore. Going up the bank into a public highway, the man placed in his hands some little articles of clothing and some bread, and then, pointing with the index finger, said: "Yonder is the North Star; you are now in a free state and may go forward; may God bless you; good-by;" and before Charley, in his astonishment, could utter a word, he was gone. A few moments the fugitive stood in a reverie which was broken by the splash of the oar in the river below, and he awoke to the consciousness that he was again alone. On the one hand was the beautiful river, whose outline he could dimly see; on the other were far reaching fields, with no habitation looming up in the darkness, and above him was the star bespangled sky, among whose myriad twinklers he looked in vain for the one which had so recently been pointed out to him. Alas, the defectiveness of his education! whilst others of his kind had been diligent in securing a definite knowledge of this loadstone of the Heavens, he had been happy in the

PLUCKY CHARLEY. 159

discharge of the light duties of his childhood home, never once thinking of flight until the fact of his sale was broken to him by his mother, and then there was no time for schooling. The dazed condition in which he now found himself from the revelations of the past hour caused him to look up to the starry firmament as into vacancy, finding nothing with which to guide himself. At length he proceeded a short distance, but becoming bewildered he sat down and soon fell asleep and dreamed that two men came and were putting him in jail. His struggles and resistance wakened him, and he set out and proceeded as best he could in the darkness. Just at daylight he espied a piece of paper nailed to a fence.

Approaching it he perceived it had upon it the picture of a negro running, and in every way looked like the one the landlord had shown him in the barn. Whilst standing thus before the picture, wrapped in thought as to what to do next, he felt a hand laid upon his shoulder, and turning saw a man with a very broad-brimmed hat and so peculiarly clothed as he had never seen one before. He was about to run when the man said: "Stop, friend, thee need not run. What have we here?" and reading the bill, he at once remarked: "Why, friend, this means thee, and thy master is ready to pay any man $500, who will place thee in his hands. Come with me or somebody may enrich himself at thy expense."

There was something so kind and frank in the

manner and words of the man that Charley followed him to a retreat deep in the woods. Seeing that he had bread with him, the stranger said: " Keep quiet and I will bring thee more food to-night," and immediately left.

As was customary in other cases, hand-bills minutely describing Charley had been widely distributed, and, of course, read by everybody, and it being a free country everybody had a right to apply the information gained as he saw fit. So it was that when Charley's master crossed into Ohio twelve hours after his chattel, and proceeded northward, he found no lack of persons who had seen just such a person that very day. Even our friend of the early morning described him minutely and had seen him wending his way into the interior only a few hours before, bearing with him a little bundle. As the route at this season of the year was supposed to be towards Sandusky or Detroit, the pursuers were decoyed on by the way of Carrollton, Allian and Ravenna towards the lake, by the smooth stories of men who had seen him only a day or two before—but only on paper. Wearied, however, they at length committed his capture to the hands of the organized set of biped hounds which infested the whole south shore from Detroit to Buffalo, and returned homeward.

When Charley's friend returned to him in the evening, he informed him of the little interview he had had with his master, and that it would be necessary for him to remain some time in his charge.

HANNAH PRAYING.

He was consequently taken to a more comfortable hiding place, and after the lapse of some three weeks was forwarded by way of New Lisbon, Poland, and Indian Run, to Meadville, and thence by way of Cambridge and Union to the parsonage at Wattsburg.

III.

The traveler who has been swept along on the Nickle Plate or Lake Shore Rail Road over the Black Swamp country and onward through Cleveland, Ashtabula and Erie, seeing little that savors of roughness, except perchance the gulches about the Forest City, the bluffs at Euclid and Little Mountain in the distance, would little think as he crosses the unpretentious bridges spanning Six-Mile-Creek, east of Erie, that just a little way back it passed through some wild and rugged country; yet such is the fact. Down through a deep gorge come its crystal waters, whilst high above them on its precipitate banks the hemlock has cast its somber shadows for centuries. Into a thin, scarcely accessible portion of this gorge came years ago John Cass, and took possession of a primitive "carding works," where he diligently plied his craft, rearing his sons and daughters to habits of industry, frugality, virtue, and a love of their little church, which is situated some two miles away on an elevated plateau, which, from its largely Celtic population has acquired the appelation of "Wales."

The little Celts of this rural community were very much surprised one winter day to see their old pastor,

Parson Rice, who resided at Wattsburg, go dashing by the school-house with a colored man in his sleigh. Never before had their unsophisticated eyes seen such a sight, and what they that day beheld was the all-engrossing theme in the homes of the Joneses the Williamses and the Davises that night.

As for Parson Rice, he kept right on down, down, until he reached the carding works of his worthy parishioner, where the woolly head of Charley was safely hidden amid fleeces of a far whiter hue.

In this retreat he remained for some time, and was taught his letters by the young Casses, William, Edward, Jane and the others. When, at length, it was deemed safe to remove him, he was taken by Mrs. Cass to the office of the *True American* in the city. From this, after a little delay, he was conveyed to the home of Col. Jas. Moorhead, who passed him on to Parson Nutting, at State Line, by whom he was duly forwarded to Knowlton Station, Westfield, New York.

Though the temperature was below zero, it was again getting hot for Charley, for vigilant eyes all along the line were watching for the young nigger whose return to his master was sure to bring $500, and that he had reached the lake shore was now a well ascertained fact, and unusual activity was noticed among the kidnapping crew.

It was a bitter cold day, with the snow flying and drifting, that Mr. Knowlton's spanking team of jet blacks, still well remembered by many a Westfielder,

PLUCKY CHARLEY.

came out of his yard attached to a sleigh, in the bottom of which was a package evidently of value, as it was carefully covered with blankets and robe. Under a tight rein the team headed eastward, and with almost the fleetness of the wind passed Portland, Brocton, and turning at the old Pemberton stand, in Fredonia, made Pettit Station. Here Charley was made safe and happy for the night, and the next day was landed safely in the Queen's Dominion from Black Rock.

CHAPTER VIII.

STATIE LINES.

I.

IT was in the decade of the forties that an enterprising farmer, named Barbour, of the Empire State, said to his neighbor, "Smith, I've a project in my head."

"Nothing strange in that," was the response; "I never knew the time when you didn't have one; but what is it?"

"Well, you know I spent a few days about Washington recently, and I believe there is money to be made in going into its vicinity and buying up some of the worn-out farms and applying to them our agricultural methods, and raising products specially for the city market."

"What can they be purchased for?"

"Anywhere from $5.00 to $10.00 an acre, any amount of them. I tell you there's money in it."

"But it would be to ostracise one's self. You know that there they consider it a disgrace for a white man to labor."

"All right. All I propose is head work."

"How is that? Democrat as you are, I don't believe you would go so far as to invest in slaves."

"No, indeed. I am fully satisfied that slavery is the curse of the South, yet it exists there, and I am bound to make some money out of it and its fruits. You see the land has been rendered worthless by slave labor in the hands of the masters, hence the extremely low price of it. As a result of the deteriorated condition of their farms, the owners of slaves are now hiring them out for wages which range much lower than with us here in New York. Whilst loathing slavery in the abstract, I confess I propose to use it for a while on wages, if some of my neighbors will join me in a purchase, so we can have a little society of our own. Will you take a hand, Smith?"

"I'll think of it."

As a result of the above conversation there were purchased in a few weeks seven or eight worn-out farms in the immediate vicinity of Washington, and in a short time they were occupied by as many sterling families from Onondaga county, N. Y. Modern methods of agriculture were applied, fertilizers were abundantly used, and though slave labor was extensively employed the fields soon yielded luxuriantly, and everything was at high tide with the newcomers, disturbed only by the twinges of conscience at the employment of southern chattel.

Among those who furnished these, was a Mr. Lines, residing just across the Potomac, in Virginia. Of him Mr. Barbour hired a number of slaves, among them a woman named Statie, nearly white, who was the mother of an amiable little girl six or seven years of age, bearing a close resemblance to the children belonging in the Lines mansion. This woman had the privilege of hiring herself out on condition of paying her master $10 per month and clothing herself and child. This she did cheerfully, laying by what she could, under the hope of being able ultimately to buy the freedom of her little girl, Lila, who was permitted to be with her at Mr. Barbour's where mother and child were both very kindly and considerately treated.

The excellent qualities of Statie as a cook having been noised about, her services were sought for a Washington hotel where much higher wages were paid than Mr. Barbour could afford and he advised her to go, as a means of the sooner freeing her child, which was consequently transferred to the home of her *owner*, where her services could now be made of some little avail.

At the end of a quarter Statie was permitted to visit home, where she soon learned through a fellow slave that a dealer had been negotiating for Lila and that at his return in a few weeks a price was to be fixed and he was to take her. The heart of the mother was wrung with agony, but the soul of the heroine rose triumphant and she went into the presence of Mr. Lines with a smile upon her face and the cheery words, "Here, Master, are your thirty dollars, and I've half as many laid by for the purchase of Lila," upon her lips.

"Indeed, Statie, you've done well. It won't be long till I'll have to give the little doll up if you go on at this rate."

"I hope not, master, for I long to see the darling with her free papers in hand."

With a lying effort, the master replied, "I hope you may succeed, for I would much sooner sell her to you than to any one else, and I shall wait on you as long as possible."

Expressing her thanks for what she knew was a hypocritical promise, Statie asked that the child might be allowed to accompany her to the capital for a few days, a request readily granted by Mr. Lines that he might the more easily avert any suspicion of his real purpose.

Cutting short her visit, Statie soon started with her child for the city, but walked several miles out of her way to lay her troubles before Mr. and Mrs. Barbour, who were greatly shocked at the revelation. Though depreciating anything in the line of *underground* work, Mr. Barbour, to whom Lila had specially endeared herself by her childish ingenuousness, after a few moments reflection said, "Wife, you know I propose making a journey across Pennsylvania soon to the vicinity of our old home. Will there be any harm in my seeing that Lila gets there?"

"No, husband; and you have my permission to see that Statie goes too. I don't think your politics ought to cripple your humanity, much less your religion. *Do unto others as ye would that they should do unto you.*"

Mr. Barbour's mind was soon made up, and Statie was dismissed with instructions to meet him on a by-road a little way out from the old north burial ground soon after dark on the Wednesday evening following.

In arranging for his proposed trip, Mr. Barbour had provided himself with a good team and a "Jersey wagon" well covered with oil cloth, supported by bows. In this wagon he placed a high box so cut down in front as to furnish a seat for himself, and so arranged that a person could sit upright in the hinder part with feet projecting forward. To the rear of this box, were attached doors, secured by a padlock whilst a good supply of straw, clothing and provisions were placed within. When all else was ready, the Jersey was labeled "Clocks," and Wednesday night Mr. Barbour drove out to the point of rendezvous where Statie and Lila were found waiting, they were immediately placed in their extemporized *retreat* and the unique emancipation car moved northward across the hills of Maryland at a rapid rate.

II.

It was court time in Warsaw, N. Y., and a large number of people were gathered about the principal hotel when a man holding the reins over a spanking team drove up and ordered accommodations for the team and himself. Beckoning the hostler forward he proceeded with the team. As he passed, a bystander remarked, " A right, royal team, that."

"Pretty good for a peddler," remarked another.

"Do you call that man a peddler?" queried a third.

"Didn't you see 'Clocks' on the cover?" came back from No. 2.

"No, indeed," was the reply, "I was too intent in looking upon the horses to notice anything else. Some down easter I suppose; sold out his load over among the pennymights, and is now on his way home likely."

Breakfast over the traveler inquired of the landlord if he knew one Col. C. O. Shepard, of Attica.

"Very well," was the reply, "he is here attending court."

"I shall be glad to see him. As he is a stranger to me, you will please call him in."

The Colonel soon appeared when the stranger said, "This is Col. Shepard, I believe."

"Shepard is my name, but I have not the honor of knowing you, sir."

"It is not essential that you should; to me it is politic you should not. I wish to make a little consignment to you," saying which he led the way to the barn, followed by the Colonel and a number of by-standers, where he opened a box in his vehicle from which emerged a well-formed octaroon woman of some thirty summers and a sprightly girl, white as any in the homes of Warsaw. At the sight of these there went up a rousing three times three, at the conclusion of which the stranger said, "These, gentlemen, are what among my neighbors are called chattel and treated as such, and that with my tacit endorsement, at least. Ten days ago if any man had told me I would assist one to escape, I should have laughed him to scorn; but when this poor woman who had worked faithfully in my family to earn the wherewith to buy the freedom of her own flesh and blood, which, against honied professions to the contrary from him who should have been the innocent one's firmest protector, was about to be sold into an ignominious servitude, came to me and pleaded for the deliverance of her child and my wife quoted, 'Do unto others as ye would that they should do unto you,' my sense of right and humanity rose above all political antecedents and predilections and here I am. Since leaving the Potomac, no human eye has looked upon these beings but mine until this moment. My affiliations and the fact it was well known I was coming north on business will shield me from suspicion, therefore ask no questions. To the direct care of Colonel Shepard, of whom the slave-owners in Dixie well know and to the protection of you all, I now consign them, trusting that no *master's* hand shall ever again be laid upon them."

There was again vociforous cheering, at the conclusion of which Col. Shepard said, "We accept the charge and I ask as a special favor that you give me the box in which you have brought them thus far on their way, as a kind of memento," a request that was readily acceded to, and in a few minutes a Jersey

STATIE LINES. 171

wagon labeled " Clocks " was speeding rapidly eastward, whilst in a day or two the box and its former occupants were taken triumphantly to Attica, the home of Col. Shepard.

III.

The time was when every person holding an office under the general government was supposed to be in sympathy with the slave power and ready to obey its behests, an idea somewhat erroneous. It was under such impressions that two strangers rode up to the post-office in the village of Attica and inquired for the postmaster. On that functionary's presenting himself they inquired if he knew anything of a slave woman, nearly white, with her little girl, being in the neighborhood, as such persons had recently escaped from the vicinity of Washington, and were believed by them to be in the immediate vicinity.

The postmaster invited them to alight and come inside, which being complied with, he said, "Gentlemen, the persons you seek are within a half mile of you, but though I might under some circumstances be willing to assist you, my advice is, let them alone. Every man, woman and child in the town is ready to protect them. You can not raise men enough in this county to secure their apprehension. I see by the commotion in the street the people are apprehensive of mischief. Such a thing as an abduction has never been attempted here, and if you are wise you will not attempt one now. Indeed

I would not like to guarantee your limbs or life fifteen minutes longer."

Beholding the commotion, the would-be kidnappers quickly mounted their horses and rode silently out of town, no demonstration being made by the multitude until the meddlers reached the bridge, when cheer on cheer arose, causing them to put spurs to their horses and get quickly out of sight, notwithstanding their threats to secure their prey, a thing they never attempted.

Statie died within two years after her escape; Col. Shepard long kept the box in which she was brought off as the only "through car" he had ever seen; Lila is still a resident of the Empire State, whilst Mr. Barbour, having disposed of his real estate sought a clime more congenial to his sense of justice and humanity.

CHAPTER IX.

GEORGE GRAY.

I.

"MY deah chile, 'tis too bad."

"Too bad, mother! I tell you I's agoin' to run away. Ole Massa can't whip dis chile no moah. I'd rather be shot or hab the dogs tear me to pieces."

"Hush, chile, hush! you'll break your ole mudder's heart, 'cause its a most done gone smashed afore, an' now she knows you can neber, neber, get across the big river an' de great lake. I tell yer, chile, you better stay wid ole mas'r if em do whip."

"Mother, my mine is made up. Masssa Jones hab whipped George Gray for de las time. I hate to leave you, mother, but then I's agoin.' Some day de Massa'll sell me as he did father an' de res' of us down South, an' then you shall see George no moah, an' I'd hab no blessed chance for 'scape, so now I's goin' for freedom or I's goin' to die. I say ole massa can't whip me no moah."

"De will ob de Lor' be done, chile; but how is you agoin' to do it?"

"I'll tell you mother, ole Masa'll neber s'pec' you, He'll neber look for George 'bout dis shanty. So I's agoin' down to de river an' cross down in de skiff, den I goes to de swamp an' comes carefully back an' crawls under your bed. When Massa misses me, you can tell him I's runned away, an' he'll start the horses an' the men for de swamp, an' for two or three days they'll hunt for George there jus' as they did for Uncle Pete; den Massa'll put me in de papers as a runaway nigger, an' then when all is ober heah I's comin' out an' goin' at de river an' cross de mountins till I gits to Canidy."

"De bressed Lor,' an' doan yer s'pec' ole Massa'll hunt dis shanty frough an' frough, chile?"

"Ole Massa'll never s'pec' you, mother; you's been wid him too long. He never whipped you, an' when he comes in de mornin', for to inquire, you mus' be prayin'; prayin 'for me that I may be cotched."

"Bress de Lor', he mus' 'ov put all dis in de head of de chile as he put his son Moses in de bullrushes down dar in de lan' of Canin. Chile, your black ole mudder'll cover you wid her bed like as the ole black hen covers her chicks when de hawk comes to steal de little ones from dar muder's lub. Now, chile,' jus' you fix it all up an' de Lor' ob dat big feller, Sabot, yes dat was de man, be wid you, an' it doan matter bout dis ole woman no moah."

The above conversation took place many years ago in a cabin in the negro quarter of the plantation of Samuel Jones on the James river, in Virginia. Mr. Jones was a thriving planter and an extensive dealer in slaves. Though in some respects of the better class of slave-breeders, he inherited many of the legitimate characteristics of the peculiar institution. Towards the men slaves he was tyranical in the extreme, whilst eyeing the fairer and younger among the women with an eye of lechery.

The plantation had come to him from his father, and with it the family of John Gray consisting of himself and wife, known for miles around as " Prayin' Hanner," and several children. The father and older children, all having a slight tinge of the Caucassion about them, Mr. Jones early sold to southern dealers, retaining only the mother and her infant George.

The mother, on account of her acknowledged piety and ability to labor, was assigned a special cabin and for years had done the family laundry work and baking and discharged other duties of a similar character. Resigned to her condition, she labored on year after year, ever singing and praying and with her loyalty all unquestioned. Not so with her growing boy, however. The white blood that was in him, though limited, constantly rebelled against his condition, and as his years advanced, brought on frequent conflicts between him and his master, which invariably ended in the boy's being severely whipped. Though feeling for him, on such occasions, as only a mother can feel, still Hannah Gray exhorted him to be obedient and submissive. Whenever the master threatened to sell him south, then it was that her prayers that one of her kin might be left to her mightily prevailed. The natural adaptability of the youth secured for him many privileges, and he had been with his master several times to the national capital and other points and had picked up much general intelligence, and his mode of expression had, to some extent, risen above the plantation vernacular.

The conflict on this particular occasion had arisen between master and slave because George had asked the privilege of visiting a young quadroon of the plantation on whom Jones had fastened his lecherous eyes. As usual the controversy ended in the young man's being bound to a post by some of the hands and then inhumanly flogged by his owner. Stung to madness, when all were settled for the night, he left his quarters and sought the cabin of his mother, and there, as we have seen, divulged his determination to seek a land of freedom. True to his purpose, when he had gained his mother's consent, he went down to the river and unloosing a skiff floated down with the current some distance and then landing, struck boldly across to a neighboring swamp. Entering this, he passed on a short distance until he came to a small creek which led directly to the river. He now divested himself of his clothing which he safely placed upon his shoulders, and following the cove soon reached the river into which he plunged, and being an expert swimmer, was soon on the home side again, and making his way quietly to his mother's cabin, where he was safely secreted beneath what he had augured an impregnable citadel, her bed.

Morning came soon, and the hands sallied from their quarters but with them came no George Gray. The word spread rapidly and soon reached both the cabin of Prayin' Hanner and the mansion that he was missing. As soon as the proprietor could dress himself and make proper inquiries, he hastened to the shanty of the mother whom he found at her morning devotions, having begun them just as she saw his approach. Not wishing to disturb her he stopped before the door and caught these words of invocation:

"Bressed Lor', dey say my poah, dear chile am gone. Am he drown? may de Lor' raise de body up dat dis ole black form may follow in its sorrow to de grabe. Hab he killed hisself? may de Lor' hab mercy on his soul, for Geog' was a bad boy; he made mas'r heaps o' trouble. O Lor', if he hab runned away, may mas'r cotch him agin—not de houn', but mas'r an' de men, an' den when mar's Jones whip him, may de bressed Lor' sen' down ole Lija, an' 'vert his soul, dat he no moah disrember mas'r but dat he do his will for his ole mudder's sake, an' for de sake ob his good mas'r, an' for de sake ob dat heben whar de Lor' is. Dis, Lor', am de prayer of poah ole Hanner, amen."

The prayer ceased and the master entered, only to find, as he inferred from it, that the intelligence of George's departure had preceded him, and farther that the boy had been in there the night before and acted very strangely; that the mother had advised him to go to his quarters and be a good boy.

Leaving the woman to her work, he went out and gave orders for a search. Soon it was discovered that the skiff was gone and directly after it was found half a mile down the river with footsteps leading towards the swamp. A pack of hounds belonging on a plantation below was sent for and search begun in earnest, and kept up unceasingly for three days but without success, and then the hands were called in. In the meantime there appeared in the Lynchburg *Herald* the following:

$500.00 Reward.

"RUN AWAY from the subscriber, George Gray, a negro, nearly pure, about twenty-one years old, and weighing one-hundred and fifty pounds. He talks pretty good English. Five hundred dollars will be given for him alive." SAMUEL JONES.

Antwerp, Va., June 25, 1841.

During these days the cabin of Prayin' Hanner was filled with sacred songs, earnest prayers and sympathizing visitors, not one of whom, white or black, as he listened to, or participated in the devotions, supposed for one moment that he who had called them all forth, that "deah chile," was quietly drinking them in. When the nights came, and everything was still, then George emerged for a little time to rest and refresh himself.

Thus matters passed until the fourth night came. The sun set amid gathering clouds. The returned hunters gathered in their quarters, some of them to

GEORGE GRAY'S ESCAPE.

tell how earnestly they had sought to find nothin'; others to depict their true loyalty to Mar's Jones, and the whites in their homes around, to swear vengeance on every nigger caught fleeing. As the storm broke and the darkness became more intense, George came forth. A little bundle of clothing, with three days' rations of food, had been carefully prepared for him. There was an embrace, tender as though the participants had been free, a "God bless you, Mother," a "May de Lor' still be wid yer as he hab bin," uttered as earnestly as though by cultured lips, and mother and son parted, never to see each other again.

George Gray went forth fearlessly into the darkness. The country he knew for miles around, and for weary hours he made his way directly up the south bank of the James. Long after midnight the moon arose, and seeking a fitting place, he crossed the river and just as the first gray streakings of the dawn appeared, quietly secreted himself in a jungle of bushes upon the mountain which here comes down close to the river. The rain had obliterated all traces of his course; he was thought to have gone in an opposite direction four days before. Thus far his plans had worked admirably, and feeling safe, he partook of his rations and lay down to a refreshing sleep.

Night found him again in motion, and by the time morning came he had made considerable progress. Again he rested and refreshed himself, and quietly surveyed the prospect for the future. He knew he was a long way from the Ohio; that much of the way was wild and mountainous, and that wherever there were people the dangers were greatest. His little stock of provisions would soon be gone, and then the berries and fruits of the forest would be his almost sole dependence, only occassionally he might go down to some bondman's cabin. With these facts before him he faltered not, but pressed resolutely forward, only to find as he approached the river, after weary weeks of vigil, that his master's advertisement had preceded him, and that base men were watching that they might claim the reward. This news came to him from colored men whom he occasionally contrived to see, for the great humanitarian thoroughfare of the days *ante bellum* had its ramifications among the mountains of Virginia, as well as its broader lines on freer soil, though unlike those of the latter their officers were of somber hue. Taken in charge by one of these, George was safely put across the river one stormy night, and in care of a genuine " broad-brim conductor " on a main trunk line, but not until his presence had been scented by a pack of white bloodhounds all too anxious for the recompence of reward, and whose unholy avarice was equalled only by the wary alertness of the disciple of George Fox.

II.

"O for a thousand tongues to sing
 My great Redeemer's praise;
The glories of my God and King,
 The triumphs of His grace."

Thus sang Azel Tracy as he stood running a wheel in his little shop in Hartford, Ohio. The last words were uttered in a subdued tone. This done, the air was continued in a fine specimen of genuine Yankee whistling, intermingled with occasional snatches from "China," or "Coronation."

It was only a sample of Mr. Tracy's *railroad* telegraphy, for the low attic of his shop, filled, in part, with bits of lumber and parts of defunct wagons, was an important *station* and it frequently became necessary to signal the waiting passengers, of whom nearly one-hundred, according to the family reckoning, found rest and protection within its narrow limits, a fact one would scarcely believe as he passes it, looking to-day almost identical with its appearance fifty years ago.

Notwithstanding Hartford is a historic anti-slavery town, there were not wanting those within its borders, who for "the recompense of reward," would willingly have divulged the presence of any fugitives in keeping had he known their whereabouts. It was to guard against this class of persons frequenting his shop that the old wagon-maker had adopted a musical system of signalizing those in his care. When any danger threatened, and silence was imperative, he would sing a snatch of some familiar hymn or whistle its air; but when "the coast was clear," Hail Columbia or Yankee Doodle was the signal for "unlimbering."

On this occasion both the words quoted and the whistling of "Old Hundred" were considered necessary as a double danger signal, for only three nights before there had climbed the narrow ladder in the corner of the shop, drawn it up and let down a board, thus completing the floor, an individual filling to a "dot" the description given in the hand-bill previously referred to, and which was already liberally scattered through Eastern Ohio and Western Pennsylvania. No questions had been asked and only necessary instructions and provisions given. Thirty-six hours later two strangers had put in an appearance in the quiet town, and soon avowed themselves as in quest of the subject of the reward offered.

They had continued to lounge about the village till this Saturday afternoon, much of the time in uncomfortable proximity to the Tracy wagon-shop, for they claimed the object of their search had been seen approaching it, and they were even now directly in its front in the highway, holding a coloquy with Dudley, the junior Tracy, and at present, 1894, the inheritor of his father's trade and shop. "Dud," as he is familiarly called, was then a strapping boy in his middle teens, bare-footed, without coat or vest, tow-headed, and to all appearances a fine subject for an interview.

THE TRACY WAGON SHOP.

SLAVE PEN IN ATLANTA, GA.
(PHOTOGRAPHED WHILST GEN. SHERMAN'S ARMY HELD THE CITY.)

"See here, boy," said one of the strangers, "have you seen anything of a young nigger about here within a day or two?"

"What do you mean, one of them black fellers like that'n the bill tells about yonder?"

"Yes, he's the chap we want to find."

"Wal, no, I hain't seen no such feller, but I hearn about him two or three days ago."

"How?"

"Why I was a layin' in the bushes up back of the church and the Gen'ral an' Sam Fuller cum along and the Gen'ral sez he, 'Fuller, that boy's got to be got off. They'r arter him.'"

"Who's the General?"

"Wal, that's Mr. Bushnell. They say he keeps some of them black 'uns some times."

"Tell us what they said."

"Wal, Fuller he said, 'What's going to be done?' and the Gen'ral said, 'You come up with the team after dark and take him down to the tow-path that's down in Pennsylvanee and tell him to keep north till he came to some colored fokeses and they'd send him to Jehu and then he'd be all right.'"

"How far is it to the tow-path?"

"O I don't know; that's on the canawl where they drive the hosses hitched to the boats, an' I never was so fur from hum."

There was some farther parlying, seemingly entirely satisfactory to the strangers, then they dropped a "bit" into Dud's hands, and under the influence of spurs two horses struck out briskly for the land of the Pennymights.

"Dud, I say Dud, come here quick," called the senior Tracy to the boy who stood gazing after the rapidly receding forms of the horsemen, and the junior slowly responded to the call.

As soon as Dud was within the door the query was raised, "What did the gentlemen want?"

"O nothing much, only they asked me if I'd seen the nigger advertised on the hand-bill yonder?"

"Well, what did you tell them?"

"O not much; I just yawned a little, telling them I heard the Gen'ral tell Mr. Fuller that he must get the boy down to Clarksville and start him north for Bishop, who would get him to the lake."

"Why, Dud, what a—"

"Come now, dad, no accusations. Didn't I just hear you tuning your gospel melody as much as to say, 'Keep still up there,' and didn't I hear you tell mother last night, when you thought we children were asleep, you didn't know what to do? But I did, and I've done it and now you needn't try to keep this thing from me any longer. You've thought I don't know what's up, but I guess I've seen the last twenty darkies you've holed in the shop and Uncle Sam has taken away, and now that I've got those fellows off, I think you can afford to let me take a hand after this."

A look of astonishment, mingled with satisfaction, overspread the countenance of Azel Tracy at this revelation of the fact that his son was acquainted with so much of the method of the *road*, a thing of which he and many another parent, for prudential reasons, tried to keep their children in ignorance, and taking the hand of the boy he replied, "You shall have all the hand in it you wish, my son."

The sun had dropped below the western horizon when the aforesaid bare-footed boy might have been seen making his way eastward to the home of farmer Fuller, bearing the following note:

48 to 1001.

Dud has cooked the goose. The feathers are left—they are good for Fennland, and the parson needs a text for tomorrow. The loft is good—the cellar better.

LEZA.

As a result of this note, when darkness had settled down upon the earth, when candles were extinguished alike in farm house and village home, the old-fashioned buggy of Samuel Fuller stood before the little Hartford shop, and Dud, the Caucassian, surrendered his seat to an African of deepest sable, and soon the vehicle was speeding rapidly northward.

III.

Night, sable goddess, had let her curtains down not only upon a day, but upon a week of toil, for the "Cotter's Saturday Night" had come to all alike, and the good people of Gustavus, Ohio, had been several hours in the Land of Nod; the dome on the old academy and the spires of the village churches were already casting moonlight shadows eastward, and good old Parson Fenn was dreaming of "Seventeenthly" in to-morrow's sermon, when there came three distinct raps upon his back door. Such signals were in no wise unusual to him, and he immediately responded to the call, only to find there a friend from fifteen miles away, and beside him a dusky figure crouching and trembling as if fearful of the moonbeams themselves.

"There's no time to be lost, Parson," said he from without. "The hounds are on the track of this game. It has only been by the most indefatigable energy that he has been kept from their grasp from the Ohio to near here. Even now they are abreast of us, only lured across the Pennsylvania line."

"He can be gotten no farther to-night," said the Parson musingly, "and all we can do is to put him in hold and keep him till the day goes by. You know the rest."

There was no word of reply, but a figure gliding silently into the street, a vehicle, with muffled wheels, was headed southward and driven rapidly away. The parson having partially dressed himself, took a jug of water from the well, a loaf of bread and a large slice of meat from the pantry and beckoning the silent figure to follow him, proceeded to a building on the northwest corner of the square, on the front of which appeared the name, "George Hezlip." Passing to the rear, he pushed aside a door. Both having entered, the door was closed, a light struck and the strange figure was soon reposing in one of several hogsheads carelessly stowed away there, whilst good Benjamin Fenn returned to his bed only to ponder on that mysterious providence which had predestined him to this materialistic work of salvation.

The Sabbath came, and with it, at the appointed hour, the people to the village church. The pastor preached with great power from the words, " Proclaim liberty throughout the land, to all the inhabitants thereof."

That sermon was long a matter of comment among the people, a balm to some, a firebrand to others, according to the political faith they entertained, but orthodox to us all after the lapse of many years.

The services ended and dinner over, the Parson sat down to his study-table and penned the following:—

5—9—081—1001—S——s——g.

XXX. In Rome when the white rabbit hangs high the Prætor leads the Vestal band by linden fields, that he may hear the tuning of the great profaner's voice ere the game goes to Quintus Anno Mundi.

49—1001—U.g.r.r.

The note thus written, was sealed and given to a trusty lad who soon placed it in the hands of an athlect, theological nimrod living in the village, whose love of humanity and admiration for universal redemption were only equalled by that of his affection for his dog, his gun and fishing tackle. When he had read the note, he bade the messenger tell the

Parson "When the stars are out," and proceeded at once to change his Sunday garb for a hunting suit.

The bell had already rung for the evening service, and the villagers and the country folk were thronging to the church when two horsemen, on jaded steeds, came down from the north and reigned up at the tavern across from Hezlip's store and requested refreshments for themselves and horses. The animals were taken in charge by the hostler whilst the riders proceeded to the bar-room and washed and cleaned themselves from the effects of their dusty ride.

Waiting supper, they had a private interview with the landlord in which they stated that they were in pursuit of a young negro who had crossed the Ohio river a few days before and been secreted by an old Quaker. They had traced him as far north as Hartford. There they had been decoyed into Pennsylvania whilst they believed that the fugitive had been run into a line farther west. After going as far north as Espyville they had come across to see if they could not regain the trail.

They were informed, in return, that there were persons in the neighborhood in the employ of the Underground Railroad, of whom the old Parson was the chief, and that it was thought from the energy with which he had preached that morning that there must be a passenger somewhere about. At the least, Boniface assured the officials, for such they had avowed themselves, that after supper he would show them one of the company's waiting rooms which he had accidentally discovered.

Twilight had deepened into evening; the "Gustavus House" bell was ringing refreshments for two, and Parson Fenn was praying fervently, "Lord, send sure deliverance to him that fleeth from oppression, and bring to naught the efforts of them that pursue for blood money," just as a square-rigged form, with elastic step, and showing great power of endurance stepped into the rear of the Hezlip building. Shoving open the door the man uttered a low whistle which was immediately responded to, and a dusky form emerged from one of the hogsheads and followed the leader without a word. Passing through the fields a short distance, they crossed the public highway beyond the churchyard and took to the woods on the right. With rapid strides they passed across fields and through forests for several miles until, leaving the little hamlet of Lindenville to the right, they descended to the Pymatuning flats where the guide deposited his ward in one of those little "hay barns," so common on the Reserve forty years ago. Returning by the home of the owner, whom he signaled at his bedroom window, he left the laconic instruction, "Feed the yearling steer," and pressed rapidly on to regain his home, which he did shortly after midnight.

Supper ended at the tavern, the host took a lantern and led his guests across the street to the basement of the store, where the jug, emptied of its contents, and fragments of the bread and meat were readily found, and an accidental application of the hand to the inner surface of the extemporized bed-room showed it still warm from the contact of human flesh.

The language which escaped the foiled pursuers when they found how near they had probably been to the object of their pursuit, was far more forcible than classic. They would have instituted a pursuit at once but Boniface told them such a thing would be useless there, for the old Parson, who was expounding Calvanism across the way, and a young Universalist in the village, who were perfectly at logerheads on matters of theology, were so in unison on the matter of running off fugitives that they would make it hotter than —— for any one who should assist them, as the most of the community were on the side of the "road." He advised that they go to Ashtabula, where the runaway would probably take boat for Canada, as their best plan.

This advise they accepted, and after a night's rest and some observations made about the village in the morning, they departed northward, and in due time drew up at the "American" in Jefferson where their presence soon attracted the attention of a "road official."

Having breakfast, our liberal theologian sauntered through the village, taking in the dimensions of the strangers and noting their departure northward, then, waiting until the sun had passed the meridian, he took his gun upon his shouldar and struck eastward as though meaning to make the Kinsman forests. Reaching a convenient point, he changed his course, and an hour before sunset threw down a half dozen squirrels upon the doorstep of the man whose slumbers he had disturbed the previous night. There was a little good-natured parleying as to who should dress the game, then busy hands were at work, and as the sun sank behind the western woodlands the family and hunter-guest sat down to a feast that would have tempted the appetite of a king.

Supper over, the guest challenged the host to take him to an appointment he had a few miles north, which was acceded to, and whilst the latter was getting ready the former went on the way a little to look after a *trap* he had set sometime before. An hour later and a vehicle with two men in the seat and a straw-covered bundle beneath was driven rapidly towards Jefferson. Arrived within a mile of the town, a halt was called under cover of a little clump of trees, one of the men alighted and stirred up the straw from which emerged a human figure. These two took a field path to the village, whilst the driver turned a little out of the public highway to await returns.

Twenty minutes later there was a rap at the side door of bluff Ben Wade's home.

"Who the d—l is there?" said a gruff voice from an upper window.

"'Thribble X' from 'A Thousand and One,'" was the quick response.

"What the h—l do you want at this time of night."

"I have a white rabbit."

"Take the black k—ss to Atkins; he'll stuff his hide."

A half hour more and the "white rabbit" was stowed in the capacious garret of "Anno Mundi" and "Thribble X" was being driven at a gay pace toward the confines of Old Trumbull.

IV.

A company of persons awaiting a western bound train stood chatting with the veteran Seely upon the platform at Girard, Pa. Among them, evidently well up in the sixties, was a man of unusually muscular frame. His countenance was open and pleasant, but mostly enveloped in a heavy beard of almost snowy whiteness. Judging from the appearance of his eyes, he was endowed with a more than average gift of language. Indeed he was the central figure in the company. The "Toledo" rolled up and as the group passed into the coach a colored man seated a little back took a close survey of this individual. As they seated themselves in his rear, the negro arose, passed to the front of the car and turning round placed his eyes squarely upon the face of the old gentleman. Thus he stood until Springfield was passed, until Conneaut was nearly reached. Feeling annoyed himself, and noticing that the gaze was attracting the attention of his fellow passengers, the gentleman arose and going forward said:

"Stranger, let us have this out. I can tolerate this impertenence no longer."

"No 'pertenence, massa, no' pertinence at all," responded the negro, "I knowed yer the minit yer commed aboard."

"You know me? I never saw you before that I remember."

"Bery like, bery like, massa, you's named Shipman, and doan yer remember the 'white rabbit' yer crawled on the hands and knees wid through the tater patch arter you'd got him out of the cellar whar the old Parson had stowed him. Dis chile hab never forgot that face though it had no whiskers then. The Lor' bress yer, massa, doan yer member so long ago?" and the overjoyed man held out his hand which was grasped in a hearty shake by that of his whiter brother.

Seating themselves together, the colored man told the story of his early servitude, and how, armed with no weapon but a butcher knife for defense, he had made that long flight across the mountains without one sense of fear until he had crossed into Ohio and learned that men were there watching for him to claim the reward offered for his return.

"But how," queried the venerable Shipman, "did you get along after I left you?"

"Lor' bress you, massa, de next mornin' that ole swearer, Massa Wade, he comed over to dat Massa Atkins an' he say, 'Doan sen' dat black k—ss to de harb'r, kase h—ll's a watchin' for him.' So dey sen me on anuder road to Erie an' put me on the 'Thomas Jefferson,' the name of that great author of *liberty* from ole Virginy, and soon I was safe in Canidy."

"And what then?" said Uncle Charley.

"An' den, Massa Shipman, George Gray went to work to earn money to buy his old mother, but when he had enough he learned she was dead, so he bought him a little home, and then the great wah comed and set all his people free, an' so now he's jus' agoin' down inter that country to see if Massa Jones hab eber heard from dat 'deah chile' who was 'drown,' or 'killed hisself' or 'runned away.' But here am my stoppin' place, an' may the good Lor' bress and save Massa Shipman forever, am the prayer ob de White Rabbit."

There was another hearty hand-shaking, amid the cheerings of the little throng who had been attentive listeners to the conversation, mutual pledges to meet on the "other shore," and the old ex-conductor from "station 1001, U. g. r. r.," and his sable passenger parted company under far pleasanter circumstances than they did in the long ago on the door-step of Anno Mundi in the village home of Giddings and Wade.